The United States
and Cuba

The United States and Cuba

From Closest Enemies to Distant Friends

Francisco López Segrera

Translated by Margot Olavarría

ROWMAN & LITTLEFIELD
Lanham • Boulder • New York • London

Published by Rowman & Littlefield
A wholly owned subsidiary of The Rowman & Littlefield Publishing Group, Inc.
4501 Forbes Boulevard, Suite 200, Lanham, Maryland 20706
www.rowman.com

Unit A, Whitacre Mews, 26-34 Stannary Street, London SE11 4AB, United Kingdom

British Library Cataloguing in Publication Information Available

Library of Congress Cataloging-in-Publication Data
Names: López Segrera, Francisco, 1940–
Title: The United States and Cuba : from closest enemies to distant friends / Francisco López Segrera.
Description: Lanham : Rowman & Littlefield, 2017. | Series: Latin American perspectives in the classroom | Includes bibliographical references and index.
Identifiers: LCCN 2016058327 (print) | LCCN 2016058742 (ebook) | ISBN 9781442267213 (cloth : alk. paper) | ISBN 9781442267220 (pbk. : alk. paper) | ISBN 9781442267237 (electronic)
Subjects: LCSH: United States—Foreign relations—Cuba. | Cuba—Foreign relations—United States.
Classification: LCC E183.8.C9 L674 2017 (print) | LCC E183.8.C9 (ebook) | DDC 327.7307291—dc23
LC record available at https://lccn.loc.gov/2016058327

Printed in the United States of America

Contents

Acknowledgments

I wrote this book between December 2014, after President Obama's December 17 announcement normalizing relations with Cuba, and July 21, 2015, the day after diplomatic relations were reestablished. The previous research that I carried out in 2010 at the University of California (UCR), Riverside, aided by Ronald Chilcote and Shery Lutjens, enriched by the deep knowledge of the subject by the editors of *Latin American Perspectives*, and supported by valuable suggestions and bibliographic information from Rhonda Neugebauer at the UCR library, have been key to this work. In addition, the time I spent in 2011 at the Bildner Center of the Graduate Center of the City University of New York was of great value.

I want to express my profound thanks to Juan Valdés Paz, who in February 2014 gave me all his digital archives dealing with the most current aspects of Cuban-U.S. relations, and with whom I had long conversations about the topic. To Carlos Alzugaray, who, during an extended conversation, offered me an interesting analysis of this problematic and provided me with extensive information on the subject. To Rafael Hernández, a deeply knowledgeable expert on the subject, with whom I also engaged in a dialogue and whose help has been invaluable. To my extensive and fruitful dialogues with Ramón Sánchez Parodi, whose experiences with this conflict—as head of the Cuban Interests Section in Washington, DC (1977–1989)—and his research on the subject, have made him one of the most knowledgeable experts on this topic. To Germán Sánchez, with whom I discussed some of the hypotheses of this book and who has always been a student of U.S. policy toward Cuba. To Armando Fernández, who also provided me with valuable digital information and his interesting views on the subject. To Oscar Oramas, who shared his experiences with me as Cuba's ambassador to the United Nations and Angola at key moments of U.S. policy toward Cuba, and who also offered me his digital files and points of view on these issues. To Esteban Morales, whose research on this topic is fundamental and who emailed me useful comments. To Juan Vela Valdés, who shared his digital files with me as well as his points of view. To Jesús Arboleya, who promptly sent me his articles on this subject and whom I consulted on some aspects of this research. To my undergraduate and graduate students of the Instituto Superior de Relaciones Internacionales de Cuba (Advanced Institute of International Relations of Cuba, ISRI), from the 1980s to the present, with whom I studied this issue for many years and whose analysis enriched my knowledge. I would like to thank my wife, Mireya Vilaseca González, who offered me her views during the course of my research and writing of the manuscript, which she also reviewed as an experienced editor.

I also thank my excellent editor, Miguel Riera, who urged me to finally develop these ideas into a book.

Introduction

The objective of this book is to offer an overview of the Cuban-U.S. conflict, its historical roots, its evolution during the revolutionary process, and the prospects that opened up for both countries once diplomatic relations were reestablished on July 20, 2015, after fifty-four years of hostility.

Chapter 1, "Historical Roots of the Cuban-U.S. Conflict," analyzes the policies of our northern neighbor toward Cuba before the triumph of the revolution and, subsequently, the policies of eleven U.S. administrations toward the revolutionary process between 1959 and 2015. Chapter 2, "Mutual Perceptions (1959–2015)," studies the different stages in the Cuban Revolution's foreign policy and the differing perceptions of the conflict by Cuba and the United States in each period. Chapter 3, "From Close Enemies to Distant Friends," addresses the following: What have been the main obstacles to resolving the issues in dispute between Cuba and the United States? Who are the main actors that influence U.S. policy toward Cuba? Why is it precisely now that diplomatic relations have been reestablished? What changed at the international level, in the United States, and in Cuba that made it possible to begin the process of normalization on December 17, 2014 (hereafter referred to as December 17), leading to the July 20, 2015, reopening of embassies (hereafter referred to as July 20)? What will be necessary for the restoration of relations to become a true "normalization"? What are the main areas of cooperation between the two countries?

The book also includes a chronology and a bibliography of the main sources used in this research.

The main hypotheses argued in this book are as follows:

1. Cuba was the United States' first neocolony. It represented a new model of domination and the beginning of U.S. imperial expansion in Latin America and the Caribbean and at the global level.

2. Until December 17, negotiations between Cuba and the United States were restricted to specific, immediately pressing issues—migration, South-West Africa, Central America, Elián González, and so forth—since the United States did not recognize the legitimacy and sovereignty of the Cuban state and demanded a change in the island's economic, political, and social system as a precondition for reestablishing relations.

3. Since the landmark events of December 17 and July 20, it is obvious that the U.S. government has adopted a new policy toward Cuba, which the island's government has accepted insofar as the United States has recognized the failure of its previous aggressive policy and accepted the legitimacy and sovereignty of Cuba without demanding a change of political regime. With due acknowledgment of the leading roles and boldness of Barack Obama and Raúl Castro in initiating this new path, the change was made possible by a growing consensus within U.S. and Cuban society on the unsustainability of the policy of hostility and blockade (called the "embargo" by the United States) and its negative effects on the citizens of both nations.

4. Despite the asymmetry between the two actors, both countries have much to gain from the new bilateral relationship. Cuba benefits especially in the economic sphere; and the United States, in terms of its international image and "soft power."

5. The difficult economic situation of Venezuela, Cuba's main political, economic, and trade ally, and the increasing fracturing of consensus in that country, constituted a strong incentive for the Cuban government to reestablish relations with United States.

6. The difficulties that Cuba confronts in "updating its economic model" under conditions of scant foreign investment while subjected to the U.S. blockade have been a powerful stimulus to reestablish relations.

7. The emergence and development of postneoliberal governments in the region—moderate (Brazil, Argentina, and Uruguay) or radical (Venezuela, Bolivia, Ecuador, Nicaragua, and El Salvador)—that are more or less critical of traditional U.S. policy toward Latin America and the Caribbean and that reject Washington's schemes for integration such as free trade agreements, have isolated the U.S. government in the region and have led it to change its policy toward Cuba.

8. The policy change toward Cuba does not imply that the United States will stop pursuing its hegemonic interests in the region, as can be seen in its aggressive policy toward Venezuela.

9. The growing multipolarity of the world order, despite the unipolarity of U.S. military power, and the emergence of new actors such as the BRICS (Brazil, Russia, India, China, and South Africa), have decisively influenced Obama's new policy toward Cuba.

10. Cuba and the United States can go from being close enemies to exemplary friends, in a context shaped by the strategic reconfiguration of international relations following the end of the Cold War and their mutual interests. Both countries have managed to avoid nuclear war and direct conventional war. Now the challenge is to create an enduring peace.

11. In the current international, Latin American, Cuban, and U.S. conjuncture—and despite tensions that will continue to exist between the two countries—now that diplomatic relations have been restored, Cuban and U.S. interests will benefit most from advancing toward full diplomatic normalization.

12. Historic, geographic, geopolitical, and economic factors have tended to sharpen the Cuban-U.S. conflict since the triumph of the revolution. However, after the Cold War ended, the reconfiguration of the international order and of security relations between the two nations have led to changes in the domestic and international policies of both countries, creating unprecedented conditions not only for reestablishing relations as occurred on July 20 but also for normalizing them.

13. The Cuba–European Union relationship has been more triangular than bilateral, due to the weight of the links of both international actors with the United States. The restoration and normalization of Cuban-U.S. relations will imply a rapprochement with the EU and

certainly the definitive elimination of the so-called Common Position that sought to turn European policy toward Cuba into a hostage of the aggressive U.S. policy toward the island.

14. Reestablishing diplomatic relations between Cuba and the United States implies profound changes in the migration policies of both countries, the existing migration agreements between them, and the migration flows between the two nations, as well as the possible repeal of the Cuban Adjustment Act, which grants preferential treatment to undocumented Cubans who reach U.S. land.

15. The restoration of relations creates the opportunity to reenvision the potential for Cuban-U.S. economic relations, going beyond the areas most developed to date: remittances, tourism, and food products. There is also great potential in fields such as energy, telecommunications, and advanced medical products and services such as biotechnology and vaccines, among other possible areas of cooperation.

During my residencies at U.S. universities since the early 1980s, I have brought my studies of Cuban-U.S. relations up to date and written books and articles on that subject, some of which I cite in the bibliography.

Chapter One

Historical Roots of the Cuban-U.S. Conflict

The conflicts between Cuba and the United States since the Cuban Revolution have deep roots that date back to the island's rebellious history as a Spanish colony.

FROM COLONIALISM TO NEOCOLONIALISM (1510–1959)

The initial forms of dependent capitalism on the island of Cuba were the *encomienda* (1510–1550) and the *hacienda* (1550–1700).* The autonomous development that the island had achieved broke down when Spain, the metropole, recovered and strengthened its monopoly control over the Cuban colony (1700–1762). Afterward, Cuba became a slave-labor plantation economy (1762–1880), specializing in sugar. This occurred in conjunction with the international capitalist system's transition from mercantilism (1510–1762) to free trade (1762–1880), hegemonically promoted by England. Between 1880 and 1902, Cuba transitioned from Spanish colonialism (1510–1899) to neocolonialism imposed by the United States.

Cuba was the last Spanish colony in the Americas and, perhaps precisely because of this, the first U.S. neocolony. The United States

---

* The *encomienda* was a system of land grants by the Spanish Crown that included rights to tribute and forced labor from the indigenous population. *Haciendas* were large estates with diverse agricultural production.

intervened in the 1895 war against Spain, which Cuba had almost won, and snatched from Cuba its full independence. The Cuban Republic was born in 1902 but with its sovereignty undermined by the U.S. presence. The United States developed a strategy to dominate the Cuban nation through a subordinated ruling class and legal instruments such as the Platt Amendment and treaties of trade "reciprocity" that turned Cuba into a specialized sugar producer and prevented its industrialization.* The Cuban experiment thus avoided bloody guerrilla wars such as the one the United States confronted in the Philippines.† However, at the slightest questioning of this order, the United States would intervene militarily, as it did several times early in the twentieth century. The Cuban neocolonial model spread to Central America and the Caribbean with the exception of Costa Rica and Mexico, the only dissenting voice in the U.S. "backyard" until the Cuban Revolution.

U.S. policy toward its first neocolony generated its anti-imperialist opposite: the Cuban Revolution. Neocolonial policy had even prevented development through import substitution, impoverishing the masses, turning the middle classes into a proletariat, and impeding the development of a national bourgeoisie.

The weakness of Cuba's dependent bourgeoisie was the result of historical circumstances. The struggle for independence from Spain did not successfully conclude in 1825, as in continental Latin America, but in 1898. In addition, the most powerful sector of the creole oligarchy, based in the western part of the island, opposed independence because it did not want to lose the capital invested in slaves and feared a slave rebellion such as the one that had culminated in the independence of Haiti as a black majority republic in 1804. The struggle for liberation involved, on one hand, the ruin of a great part of the Cuban bourgeoisie (total destruction on the eastern side of the island, which was devastated by the fighting), because the independence wars (1868–1898) and the competition to cane sugar from beet sugar led to a process of industrial concentration that could only be confronted by the wealthiest.[1]

---

* During the military occupation of Cuba that began in 1898, the United States imposed the Platt Amendment on the Cuban constitution of 1901, granting the United States the right to intervene in the island's internal affairs and obligating the Cuban state to cede bases for U.S. ships. One of those bases was Guantánamo, which the United States has maintained until the present.

† The Philippines became a U.S. colony after the Spanish American War. Resistance to U.S. rule led to the Philippine-American War of 1899 to 1902.

On the other hand, the independence struggle encouraged the oligarchical interests of the surviving sector of the Cuban bourgeoisie to form an antinational coalition with the powerful U.S. sugar interests, which offered them better prospects for profits than did the Spanish market. These interests at first welcomed the intervention of emerging U.S. imperialism at the end of the 1895 war, which the different sectors of this privileged corporate bloc had consistently called for. Later so did the government of Cuba's first president, Tomás Estrada Palma. This facilitated the integration of the Cuban economy into the U.S. market and the rapid increase of enormous U.S. investments.

The great weakness of the Cuban bourgeoisie in the 1930s, and specifically of its industrial sector, prevented it from retaining power after the Revolution of 1933 overthrew the dictator Gerardo Machado. This weakness was reinforced by the large amount of U.S. capital in Cuba and the role the imperial center assigned to the neocolony as a consumer of its manufactured products and as a sugar producer. The new but short-lived Ramón Grau–Antonio Guiteras government was inspired by an industrial-nationalist ideology, similar to the one that came to power in other Latin American countries at that time. Once again, the diminished, privileged, corporate Cuban-U.S.-Spanish bloc favored imperialist intervention (under U.S. ambassadors Summer Welles and Jefferson Caffery) that was supported, as before, by the local governing agents (Carlos Céspedes, Carlos Mendieta, and Fulgencio Batista) who served corporate interests. These interests definitively coincided with those of imperialism, thus frustrating the revolutionary process that began in 1933.

The strong man in Cuban politics between 1934 and 1944 was army chief of staff Colonel Fulgencio Batista, who enjoyed the unconditional support of the armed forces, the oligarchic bloc, and the U.S. embassy. He held power behind the scenes between 1934, when he overthrew Ramón Grau in a counterrevolutionary coup, and 1940 through a series of presidents (Mendieta, 1934–1935; José Barnet, 1935–1936; Miguel Mariano, 1936; and Laredo Bru, 1936–1940), who served as his compliant puppets. Between 1934 and 1937, he carried out bloody military repression against all the revolutionary forces that aspired to break free of the neocolonial relationship.

Land use clearly reveals Cuba's social structure from 1900 to 1930. While nonsugar agriculture occupied more or less the same land area (1,050,000 hectares or 2,594,606 acres) as did the sugar monoculture, it did not have the same economic importance as sugar cane, which qualitatively dominated the Cuban economy. According to the 1929 census, it represented 67.81 percent of national agricultural production, compared to 10.5 percent for food products, 10.3 percent for beef, and 4.2 percent for tobacco. In 1924, sugar constituted 84 percent of exports, and in 1933, it still represented 70 percent. Both this social structure and the composition of foreign trade remained practically unchanged until the victory of the revolution in 1959.

After a weak democratic interlude between 1940 and 1952 during the presidencies of Batista, Grau, and Carlos Prío, Batista led a coup d'état, supported by the United States, the military, and sectors of the Cuban oligarchy. Armed protest against his dictatorship began when Fidel Castro led an unsuccessful attack on the Moncada barracks on July 26, 1953, for which he was tried, convicted, jailed, and subsequently exiled to Mexico. There he formed a group of revolutionaries, including Che Guevara, to return to Cuba to continue the anti-Batista struggle. Later, under his leadership of the Twenty-Sixth of July Movement, protest rose to the level of armed struggle in the cities and then guerrilla war in the countryside after his rebel forces, sailing from Mexico, landed in the rural eastern region in December 1956. Once armed protest reached almost massive proportions, the dependent Cuban bourgeoisie began to view favorably Fidel's leadership of a possible populist solution. However, the political project of the Cuban leader allowed him to transcend the populist protest of the nationalist leaders of the 1930s (Guiteras) and 1940s (Eduardo Chibás) and fully commit himself to revolutionary socialist transformation. He brought together the nationalist current—represented by José Martí, Guiteras, and Chibás—and the socialist current—represented by Carlos Baliño, Julio Mella, and the Communist Party—into a Marxist ideological synthesis. This was profoundly rooted in the national problematic and in the country's revolutionary thought, whose core theoretical nucleus, strongly influenced by Martí, was already outlined in Fidel's "History Will Absolve Me" self-defense speech at his trial (1953) for the Moncada attack.[2]

Some sectors of the middle classes participated in the insurrectionary struggle against the dictator Batista and identified themselves with the revolutionary project, the peasantry, and the proletariat, rather than with the bourgeoisie that the United States had stripped of economic, political, social, and cultural identity and that, therefore, lacked historical legitimacy.

The Cuban bourgeoisie was integrated into the U.S. neocolonial model of domination and reacted confrontationally to the revolution after its victory in 1959. The following statistics reveal the weakness of the ruling class, subordinate to the United States, on the eve of the revolution in 1958: 40 percent of sugar production, 90 percent of electric and telephone services, 50 percent of railway, and 23 percent of nonsugar industries were U.S. property. The value of U.S. capital invested in Cuba was approximately one billion dollars. In addition, U.S. companies—U.S. Rubber, Firestone, Procter and Gamble, and so forth—established subsidiaries on the island, which as a rule allowed the participation of Cuban capital only in sectors where it served the interests of U.S. capital. In the 1950s, 60 percent of Cuban exports went to the U.S. market, and 80 percent of its imports came from there.

Primary products such as sugar and tobacco were exported to the United States and manufactured goods were imported. In the period 1948–1958, the unfavorable trade balance with the United States was $603 million. These figures were the result of Cuban dependence on the United States since 1902, not only politically (the Platt Amendment), but also economically and commercially, due to the treaties of commercial "reciprocity," which turned the island into a neocolony until the revolution. This helps to explain why the U.S. blockade established in 1962 constituted a serious challenge for the survival of the revolution and explains its movement toward a very close relationship with the Soviet Union and other socialist countries.

A CHRONOLOGY OF THE CUBAN REVOLUTION

1959–1961   The initial stage lasted from the victory of the revolutionary forces over the Batista dictatorship on January 1, 1959, until the declaration of the revolution's socialist character in 1961.

1961–1970   In this phase, the revolution attempted to develop an original model.* It did not condemn the Soviet

---

* It was a nationalist revolution making decisions through consensus with popular participation in permanent interaction with the leadership and without heavy bureaucratic structures as in the Soviet model that emerged from Stalinism. After 1970 and mainly after the First Congress of the Cuba Communist Party in 1975, this original model was contaminated by the copy of the Soviet model as was later recognized.

Union's invasion of Czechoslovakia in 1968 and
failed to achieve its goal of an unprecedented sugar
harvest of ten million tons in 1970. This implied the
failure of its economic strategy. Support for tricontinental revolutionary movements in Asia, Africa, and
Latin America and the determination to construct an
original model was replaced by a closer alliance with
the Soviet Union after 1968. This did not mean subordination but involved general agreement among the
leadership to follow the Soviet model.

1970–1975   Change toward the Soviet model in the cultural sphere
was known as "the five gray years," because of the
hard-line policy applied to intellectuals. In 1975 the
First Congress of the Cuban Communist Party took
place.

1975–1986   The country attained significant economic growth and
institutional achievements, such as important military
victories in Angola and Ethiopia. However, when the
"process of rectification of errors" began in 1986,*
the system was showing signs of economic stagnation,
corruption, and crisis.

1986–1990   The "process of rectification of errors" was interrupted
in 1990 by the fall of the socialist bloc. The Special
Period began in 1990.

1990–1993   The failure of "actually existing socialism" and of the
economic relationship with the Council for Mutual
Economic Cooperation (COMECON) had a dev-
astating impact on the Cuban economy, which had
virtually no significant trade relationships with other
countries.

1993–2000   Economic reform was undertaken, a degree of economic growth was achieved, and new trade links were
established. Nevertheless, for a number of years the
main trade partner continued to be Russia, followed
by Spain, Canada, China, Latin America, and some

---

* In 1986 "rectification processes" were launched and aimed at correcting some deforma-
tions of the economic model, such as the practice of increasing salaries in factories from an
average of three hundred pesos to more than one thousand pesos because of overtime on paper
rather than real overtime hours worked.

	European countries (other than Spain). Increasing inequalities were the price paid for economic reform.
2000–2006	In the political sphere, the mass mobilization for the return of Elián González from Miami indicated a resurgence of revolutionary spirit. In the economic arena, a new policy of economic recentralization was put into practice, with the objective of dedicating enormous resources to social services (medicine, education, and aid to very low-income sectors) through special programs of the "Battle over Ideas," launched and led by Fidel Castro, with the aim of correcting inequalities generated by the economic reform. Venezuela became Cuba's main political, economic, and trade ally. In 2006, Cuba's Ministry of the Economy declared that the Special Period had ended, given the value attained by the GDP.
2006–2014	On July 31, 2006, after major surgery left him weakened, Fidel provisionally delegated the presidency to his brother, Raúl Castro. On February 24, 2008, Raúl was elected president.
2014–2015	On December 17, 2014, the Cuban and U.S. presidents announced the beginning of the process to restore diplomatic relations. They were reestablished on July 20, 2015.

The Cuban Revolution was the Cuban people's response to the contradictions created in Cuban society by the neocolonial model imposed by the United States. Politically, the expression of this model was the Batista dictatorship; in the economic realm, underdevelopment; socially, 20 percent unemployment (and a high rate of underemployment); in international relations, the absence of an independent foreign policy; and in the cultural sphere, a growing crisis of cultural identity, threatened by images of the "American way of life," despite the existence of a "culture of resistance" among some vanguard sectors on the island.[3]

Due to the U.S. economic blockade, Cuba had no option other than joining COMECON. The rupture of trade links with COMECON produced the economic crisis that Cuba faced starting in 1989.[4] Cuba partially recovered during the 1990s, but it did not achieve a GDP comparable to that of 1989 until 2006.[5]

The main challenge now—in the economic, political, social, cultural, and international spheres—is how to construct a new model of socialism to prevent Cuba's return to dependent capitalism and the prerevolutionary neocolonial model.

FROM EISENHOWER TO OBAMA (1959–2015)

Dwight Eisenhower (1959–1961) did not receive Fidel in Washington when he traveled there on a goodwill mission shortly after the revolution; instead, he designated Vice President Richard Nixon to meet with him. Eisenhower launched defamation campaigns against Cuba; formed a mercenary army under the command of war criminals from the Fulgencio Batista dictatorship (1952–1959) to invade Cuba; used CIA covert operations to promote the internal counterrevolution through terrorist acts of sabotage and attempts to assassinate Fidel Castro; and initiated the economic blockade and used the Organization of American States (OAS) for subversive purposes. On January 3, 1961, shortly before the end of his administration, the United States broke diplomatic relations with Cuba.

John F. Kennedy (1961–1963), in accordance with his spirit of a "New Frontier," developed a counterinsurgency doctrine and the Alliance for Progress as an alternative to the Cuban Revolution. On February 3, 1962, by presidential proclamation, he decreed the total embargo (blockade) of trade between the United States and Cuba. The Bay of Pigs (Playa Girón) invasion and the Cuban Missile Crisis are key events in a policy that Kennedy began to recognize as mistaken in his June 1963 speech at American University. His intention to change policy at the time he was assassinated was confirmed by his biographers Theodore Sorensen and Arthur Schlesinger. On the day of the assassination, Fidel Castro received a message from the U.S. president through the French journalist Jean Daniel intended to arrange a meeting to discuss the disagreements between the two nations.

Robert F. Kennedy Jr., the son of Robert Kennedy and nephew of the president, published three articles in December 2014 and January 2015 in which he analyzed how the CIA and powerful political forces in the United States opposed a change in President Kennedy's policy toward Cuba.[6] After the missile crisis of October 1962, which almost unleashed a nuclear cataclysm, and the resolution of the conflict by the removal of Soviet missiles from Cuba and U.S. missiles from Turkey, President Kennedy decided to embark on a process of normalizing relations with Cuba. In September 1963, Kennedy commissioned William Attwood, journalist and U.S. diplomat, to "open secret negotiations with Castro."[7] That same month, President Kennedy created "another secret channel of communication with Castro through the French journalist Jean Daniel."[8] Before traveling to Cuba to interview the Cuban first minister, Daniel met with Kennedy in the White House, and Kennedy gave him a message for Fidel. Fidel's response to Jean Daniel was the following: "I believe Kennedy is sincere, I also believe that today the expression of this sincerity could have political significance."[9] Referring to the need for a U.S. leader to understand Latin American realities, he expressed optimism that "Kennedy could still be this man. He still has the possibility of becoming, in the eyes of history, the greatest President of the United States, the leader who may at last understand that there can be coexistence between capitalists and socialists, even in the Americas. He would then be an even greater President than Lincoln."[10]

However, the CIA resolutely opposed any change in policy toward Havana. According to Attwood, the attitude of the CIA was "to hell with the president it was pledged to serve."[11] Robert Kennedy Jr. reported that after the death of President Kennedy, Fidel persistently asked Adlai Stevenson, William Attwood, and others to request Lyndon Johnson to resume the dialogue, but Johnson ignored the requests and Castro eventually stopped trying.[12]

Attwood affirmed that "there is no doubt in my mind. If there had been no assassination, we probably would have moved into negotiations leading to a normalisation of relations with Cuba."[13] After Kennedy's assassination, Fidel affirmed, "I was convinced that Kennedy was starting to change. . . . To a certain extent we were honored in having such a rival. . . . He was an outstanding man."[14]

During the administration of Lyndon B. Johnson (1963–1969), the U.S. government found its possibilities of direct aggression against Cuba limited by four factors: (1) The United States made a commitment to the Soviet Union during the missile crisis of 1962 not to carry out a direct military attack on Cuba. (2) Much of its military power was committed to the Vietnam War. (3) Cuba had achieved internal consolidation, despite the blockade. (4) And growing international solidarity, not only from socialist countries, but also from other developed and third world countries, particularly in Latin America, strengthened Cuba's position.

At the end of the Nixon (1968–1974) administration, and especially during the presidency of Gerald Ford (1974–1976), concrete positive steps were taken to improve relations between the two countries in accordance with the First Linowitz Report of 1974, which considered the policy of isolating Cuba to be contrary to U.S. interests. A bilateral agreement on airline hijacking was signed. Trade and sports contacts were established, and in August 1975 Washington lifted the prohibition on exporting products of U.S. subsidiary companies to Cuba. These contacts were interrupted due to the Ford administration's questioning of Cuba's foreign policy toward Angola and Puerto Rico.

The same reasons impeded the rapprochement that was reinitiated when Jimmy Carter (1977–1981) became president and had led to the opening of Interests Sections (1977) in both countries and other positive measures in the spirit of the recommendations of the Second Linowitz Report.

However, what really stalled the negotiating process in both administrations was that, while Cuba had always maintained that the two countries should negotiate as equals, the United States sought unilateral concessions on multilateral issues (such as Cuban-Soviet relations, Cuban policy in Africa—[Angola and Ethiopia]—and in the Caribbean Basin, and its support for revolutionary movements) before dealing with the bilateral issues of interest to Cuba.

In 1981 the main thrust of the Reagan (1981–1989) administration's policy toward Cuba was the threat of aggression. But faced with Cuba's combative stance and public and congressional opposition to a long, costly war with an uncertain outcome, in 1982 it shifted to greater emphasis on ideological war without discarding the aggressive option. Between 1983 and 1989 it focused its line of attack on other issues: opposing the negotiation of the Cuban foreign debt, restricting U.S. citizens' travel to Cuba, denying visas to Cuban officials and intellectuals, expelling Cuban representatives to the UN, developing campaigns about Cuba's alleged subversive role in Central America and the supposed violation of human rights on the island, and trying to implicate Cuba in drug trafficking and accusing it of building up its armaments with aggressive intent. Reagan also signed legislation in 1985 creating Radio Martí to broadcast from the United States to Cuba (1985) and intensified the economic blockade through an executive order on

August 23, 1986. Between 1983 and 1989 the military provocations did not cease. There were multiple violations of Cuban air space, such as that by Blackbird SR-71 reconnaissance aircraft in December 1986 and those included in the Ocean Venture military exercises in April 1984. During the U.S. invasion of Grenada (1983), Cuban personnel working on that island were attacked.

However, relations improved somewhat when the migration agreements of 1984, which had been suspended in 1985 after the creation of Radio Martí, were restored on November 20, 1987, and there were successful quadripartite negotiations among the United States, South Africa, Angola, and Cuba to deal with the situation in southern Africa.*

The administration of President George H. W. Bush (1989–1993) did not follow up on the recommendations of the Second Santa Fe Document (Sante Fe II)—withdrawal of Cuban troops from Angola, ending its influence in Central America, and distancing itself from the USSR and the Soviet bloc—for the simple reason that these priorities had already been resolved in a relatively satisfactory way for U.S. interests. The previously mentioned quadripartite agreements brought about the withdrawal of Cuban troops from Angola and the independence of South-West Africa (renamed Namibia), and there were no more debates about those issues, but contrary to some expectations, there was no progress toward negotiations on other contentious bilateral issues between Cuba and the United States. After the U.S. invasion of Panama (1989), the electoral defeat of Sandinismo in Nicaragua (1990), and the disintegration of the Socialist camp, the United States thought that the days of the Cuban Revolution were numbered in a unipolar world where it exercised an undisputed hegemonic role after the Gulf War (1991).

The reasons the United States emphasized for not changing its aggressive policy toward Cuba were issues focused on Cuban domestic, rather than foreign, policy. It wanted Cuba to move toward what the United States considered democracy, to respect human rights, and to hold elections. It hoped to change the Cuban regime by peaceful means through elections that would enshrine its concept of democracy and the market economy.

---

* In late 1988, at the request of the Angolan government, Cuba sent troops to assist Angolan forces fighting against internal rebels (UNITA) supported by South African troops. The Cubans were instrumental in defeating the combined UNITA and South African forces at the decisive battle of Cuito Cuanavale in early 1989.

Between 1989 and 1990, however, the United States exerted strong pressure on the Soviet Union to curtail its relations with Cuba, conditioning possible economic aid to the Soviet government and later to the CIS (Commonwealth of Independent States) on cutting economic and military ties with the island. After the dissolution of the Soviet Union and the emergence of the CIS, this created a double blockade—that is, the traditional U.S. blockade plus the new one by the CIS.

After the failure of the 1991 coup d'état in the then Soviet Union and the departure of the Soviet brigade in Cuba in 1992 (although Russia wanted to maintain its radio listening post at Lourdes), all that remained of the previous Cuban ties to Russia was a precarious trade relationship.

The Bush administration maintained its aggressive stance toward Cuba. It supported Radio Martí and asylum seeking by Cubans in European embassies in Cuba in order to create problems for Cuba with these countries. There were clashes in the UN over the Gulf War (1991). On October 23, 1992, the Torricelli Act was passed to tighten the blockade, and vessels with Cuban crews were attacked militarily on the pretext of drug trafficking.

However, despite this, relations between the two countries were not entirely negative during the Bush administration:

- Interests Sections were maintained.
- Migration treaties continued to be observed.
- The agreements signed after the quadripartite negotiations over South-West Africa made it clear that when the political will existed on both sides, Cuba and the United States could reach agreement on complex issues.

Especially after the collapse of the Soviet Union, the U.S. political class thought that Cuba could not survive after the loss of its economic relationship with COMECON. Bush administration policy toward Cuba was based on the assumption that the socialist system on the island would also collapse. In the scenario of Cuba without Soviet support, in which its economic viability was still to be demonstrated, it was "logical" for the United States to imagine that Cuba could be dealt with using a plan similar to the one that had succeeded in Nicaragua.

On February 27, 1992, President Bush wrote in an opinion column in the *Miami Herald*, "We have seen the collapse of communism in Europe, where the United States has played a positive role. United States policy in Eastern Europe was predicated on the fact that the Poles, the Czechs, the Germans and the other peoples in the region wanted to live in freedom. The Cubans are no different."[15]

The Democratic Party, which had dealt with Cuba during the administrations of Kennedy and Carter, returned to power with President Bill Clinton (1993–2001).

In the context of the electoral campaign, Bush expressed doubts about signing the Cuban Democracy Act, commonly known as the Torricelli Act, to tighten the blockade against Cuba. Clinton declared that he would sign it, and consequently Bush quickly did so.

In 1993 the coast guards of both countries resumed talks about professional collaboration that had been suspended since the early 1990s; that same year Cuba captured and turned over to the United States two drug traffickers. Also in 1993, the Cuban government allowed churches in Cuba—particularly the Catholic Church hierarchy—to receive millions of dollars in humanitarian aid from the United States despite the fact that the United States had tried to impede several "Friendshipment" aid caravans to Cuba organized by the progressive Protestant Interreligious Foundation for Community Organization (IFCO)/Pastors for Peace. At the end of 1994, agreements were signed with U.S. telecommunications companies, completing negotiations begun in 1993, the same year that Cuba also liberalized permits for U.S. residents of Cuban origin to visit Cuba for short periods.

Between October 1993 and July 1994, the Clinton administration continued to moderate the aggressive rhetoric of the Bush and Reagan administrations without making substantive changes to the policies initiated in the early 1970s—which Carter liberalized and the Republican presidents hardened—of negotiating with Cuba on limited bilateral issues while maintaining the blockade. Despite this, the rupture in the previous U.S. consensus supporting the "embargo" continued to widen, although it did not seem that in the short term this could lead to fundamental changes in U.S. government policy toward Cuba. Between October 1993 and July 1994, the U.S. government showed on various occasions that it would not change the essence of its policy toward Cuba. In early 1994, in a press conference on CNN, President Clinton expressed support for the Torricelli Act and stated that he did not intend to change his policy toward Cuba, asserting that whether the United States and Cuba improved relations depended on Fidel Castro and the development of democracy in Cuba. On May 20, 1994, in a four-hundred-word televised message to the Cuban American National Foundation (CANF), Clinton described the Havana regime as a "dictatorship,"[16] defended the blockade, and announced the continuation of broadcasts hostile to the Cuban government on Radio and TV Martí. The Cuban newspaper *Granma* replied with a strong editorial, and on May 26 President Fidel Castro stated that "Clinton maintains the same severity" toward the Cuban Revolution as his predecessors.[17]

The U.S. government's policy of "linkage" consisted of conditioning improved relations with Cuba on the development of a U.S.-style democracy on the island. It intended to promote a Nicaragua-like outcome in Cuba, removing the revolutionary government from power through elections.

Since the fall of the socialist bloc, Cuba had ceased to be a major foreign policy concern for the United States. The Cuban "*balsero* (rafter) crisis" of August 1994 returned it to high-priority status. Following social protests on August 4, the Cuban government announced that all those who wished to emigrate could do so freely without an exit permit. After thousands of Cubans took to the sea on rafts, on August 19 the United States canceled its traditional migration policy that automatically granted political asylum to Cubans who reached U.S. territory and began to arrest them, taking them to the Guantánamo Naval Base. Due to this migration crisis, the Cuban issue was once again perceived in Washington as a national security matter (although in different terms than during the Cold War).

On September 9, 1994, Cuba and the United States signed a migration accord, which involved the United States accepting twenty thousand legal immigrants annually, in exchange for Cuba preventing the massive emigration by sea. Under the terms of the accord, the thirty thousand Cuban refugees in Panama and Guantánamo were given the option of remaining there or returning to Cuba, where their rights would be guaranteed, but they would not be allowed to enter the United States.

Between the signing of the migration accord on September 9 and May 2, 1995, when a joint U.S.-Cuba declaration was issued, specifying and broadening its reach, several rounds of talks were held, in which both parties expressed their satisfaction with the implementation of the accords. The May 2 joint declaration established that the United States would return to Cuba all *balseros* rescued on high seas and that, on the other hand, it would allow the majority of the twenty-one thousand refugees housed at the Guantánamo base to enter U.S. territory. The objective of these accords was an orderly regulation of the migratory flow. But they maintained the Cuban Adjustment Act of 1966, through which the United States stimulated Cuban illegal immigration by granting Cuban migrants asylum and giving them privileged treatment.

Considering the social protests of 1994 and the *balsero* crisis, during a news conference President Castro analyzed how the United States had stimulated the illegal exodus and not complied with the migration accord of 1984, with the objective of producing a bloodbath in Cuba, using the blockade as the "main policy instrument that drives mass emigration."[18] According to the 1984 migration accord, the United States should have granted 164,000 visas between 1985 and 1994 but granted only 11,222, while continuing to encourage illegal emigration.

The most important result of these accords was that they tended to isolate the extreme right of the Cuban community (CANF), which opposed returning to Cuba the *balseros* who had arrived in the United States illegally. It put the issue in the hands of the Clinton administration, which at that time did not seem to be hostage to the Cuba policy of CANF or other extreme right-wing sectors in the United States. Therefore, various analysts predicted that President Clinton would veto the Helms-Burton Act written by the conservative "hawks" Senator Jesse Helms, chairman of the Senate Foreign Relations Committee, and Congressman Dan Burton, which was intended to tighten the blockade on Cuba and prevent access to investment from third countries.

However, the shooting down by the Cuban air force on February 24, 1996, of two civilian planes coming from Florida led to a hardening of U.S. policy. The planes, piloted by members of Brothers to the Rescue, a counterrevolutionary exile group based in Miami, violated Cuban air space as they had with impunity in previous raids, dropping leaflets hostile to the Cuban government on the city of Havana. What was new was the Cuban government's decision to shoot down the planes in a U.S. election year. Washington reacted immediately. In addition to retaliatory measures such as pressuring the UN Security Council to approve a statement denouncing Cuba's actions, increasing Radio Martí broadcasts, and suspending charter flights from the United States to Cuba, the main expression of hardening U.S. policy toward Cuba was signing the Helms-Burton Act on March 12, 1996. Key provisions included codifying the "embargo" into law—that is, preventing it from being lifted by a presidential executive order but requiring approval by Congress; denying U.S entry visas to persons who make or increase investments in U.S. property that had been confiscated in Cuba (Title IV); and granting all U.S. citizens who claim to have lost property in Cuba (not just the 5,911 persons or companies the United States identified at the time of the expropriations) the right to sue in U.S. courts individuals or companies that "traffic in" such confiscated properties in Cuba (Title III). The most controversial articles are those in Title III that allow the extraterritorial application of the act, although these provisions have not yet been applied. President Clinton authorized six-month suspensions in July 1996 and January 1997; succeeding presidents have not applied the provisions either.

Canada, Mexico, the European Union, the OAS, the Rio Group, and the Ibero-American Summit rejected the Helms-Burton Act for violating international law and as inhumane. The Cuban government considered the law unacceptable and, on March 23, 1996, presented a formal complaint to the World Trade Organization (WTO). In its December 1996 session, the Cuban Parliament officially rejected the Helms-Burton provisions.

The Helms-Burton Act led to contentious relations between the European Union (EU) and the United States. Clinton named the deputy secretary of the Treasury and ex-ambassador to the EU, Stuart Eizenstat, as special envoy to accomplish two objectives: grant semiannual postponements of Title III and in return obtain a tightening of EU policy toward Cuba. The Spanish government of José Aznar spearheaded the issue, resulting in the so-called Common Position that turned EU policy toward Cuba into a hostage of U.S. policy. A degree of "détente" with the United States was observed in December 1996, when dialogue on migration issues resumed. As the first joint meeting after the downing of the planes and Clinton's reelection, some interpreted it as a gesture by the United States to ease tensions, especially after it had failed to move the Cuban policy of the EU and other allies as far to the right as it desired. Another reading considered the renewal of the migration dialogue as the White House's way of continuing to implement the first track of the Torricelli Act (political and economic war against Cuba) while further developing the second track—that is, to bring about, in the medium term, the peaceful subversion of the Cuban regime from within. The plan for a "transition to democracy" in Cuba announced by President Clinton in January 1997 must be viewed in this context,[19] which also explains the president's March 20, 1996, suspension of the regulations issued in August 1994 and February 26, 1996, that blocked both charter flights from the United States to Cuba and financial remittances of up to $1,200 annually from U.S. residents to their relatives on the island. Secretary of state Madeleine Albright stated on March 20 that these measures were a U.S. gesture linked to the pope's visit to Cuba in January 1998 but also affirmed that they "do not represent a change in policy toward the Cuban government,"[20] which remained advocating a peaceful transition to democracy. She added that "the Cuban people are beginning to think beyond Castro, and we need to do the same." Nonetheless, Fidel described these measures as "positive" and "conducive to a better climate."[21] However, the support for regime change reinforced U.S. policy that had consistently been to negotiate only about limited matters in its immediate interest but not to engage in discussion of the central issues in dispute, thereby preventing significant progress toward restoring diplomatic relations.

A landmark episode was the struggle to return the young boy Elián González to Cuba as demanded by his father after his mother died at sea in an illegal attempt to reach the United States. The protracted battle lasted from November 1998 to June 28, 2000, when Elián was finally returned to Cuba. It was a beautiful episode of solidarity between Cubans and Americans and served to launch a key initiative in Cuba to strengthen revolutionary values: the battle of ideas.

To summarize, except for the period following the February and March 1996 plane downings by Cuba and the approval of the Helms-Burton Act, the migration crisis of 1994 led to "rapprochement" with the island, with U.S. policy no longer being hostage to right-wing sectors of the Cuban community. Thus, during his first administration, President Clinton was motivated to make important changes in his Cuba policy by the threat of uncontrolled migration to the United States combined with his doubts that taking a hard-line approach toward Cuba would allow him to win the upcoming presidential election in Florida (where he lost in 1992), and that the right-wing Cuban American National Foundation should remain the key lobby influencing U.S. policy. This did not mean that the Clinton government had given up its goal of finding a "solution" to the Cuban crisis through a peaceful Nicaragua-style transition. Nor had it totally or definitively discarded a direct military intervention or one using a multilateral force under the umbrella of a UN Security Council resolution in the event that an upsurge of social protest unleashed a civil war or there was another uncontrolled mass emigration, as in summer 1994. Had these scenarios occurred, the first and second Clinton administrations would have carried out a Haitian-style option (military intervention) and not a Nicaragua-style one (toppling the revolution through elections). At no time did military intervention appear likely, since Europe (various European countries already had important investments and growing trade with the island by that time) and even broad sectors in the United States desired a smooth transition of Cuban socialism as had occurred in Eastern Europe. Moreover, the United States knew that Cuba was prepared for conventional war and a protracted people's war according to the doctrine of War of the Whole People (Guerra de Todo el Pueblo, GTP). This doctrine involved relying only on its own forces and logistics in case of a military attack, giving special weight to ground forces rather than sea or air power, and reinforcing the armed forces by incorporating all of Cuban society organized through territorial and other militias to resist the invader. Originally it had been formulated during the Reagan era and was adapted to Cuba's new situation at the beginning of the 1990s, which required reducing its armed forces.

From 1998 through the end of his term, there was some liberalization in Clinton's Cuba policy. Nonetheless, despite some ups and downs, hostile policy was a constant during his presidency. This was demonstrated in 1997 by terrorist attacks against tourist facilities in Havana and Varadero organized by the anti-Cuban mafia residing in the United States, linked to CANF. One of these attacks took the life of the young Italian Fabio Di Cemo. In June 1998 FBI agents met with Cuban specialists in Havana, who turned over considerable evidence of terrorist actions against Cuba planned in the United States and expressed willingness to collaborate to stop them. The U.S. response was the September 12, 1998, arrest of the undercover agents Cuba calls the Five Cuban Heroes (known in the United States as the Cuban Five), antiterrorist operatives who served harsh sentences in U.S. prisons, while terrorists such as Luis Posada Carriles (responsible for bombing a Cuban civilian airliner in 1976 as it left Barbados killing all aboard) freely walked U.S. streets. Additional evidence of the Clinton administration's hostile policy were the attempts on Fidel Castro's life during the Latin American Summits held in Venezuela in 1997 and in Panama in 2000.*

On July 13, 2001, George W. Bush (2001–2009) announced a series of measures intended to tighten the blockade. On September 20, 2001, in comments on the twin towers' attack, Bush identified Cuba as a state sponsor of terrorism, launching a veiled threat of military attack. On May 6, 2002, the undersecretary of state, John R. Bolton, declared, "The U.S. believes that Cuba has at least a limited offensive biological warfare research and development effort. Cuba has supplied dual-use biotechnology to other rogue states."[22] In April 2003, secretary of defense Donald Rumsfeld threatened a military attack on Cuba if it developed weapons of mass destruction.

The Commission for Assistance to a Free Cuba (CAFC) created by President Bush on December 5, 2003, produced at his direction two Reports to the President (known in Cuba as Plan Bush I and II) that defined relations with Cuba during his administration. The commission, composed of high officials from several government departments, was charged with formulating "transition" plans "to plan for the happy day when Castro's regime is no more and democracy comes to the island."[23]

The 2004 report, in the context of euphoria over the Iraq War, aimed to remove Cuba's socialist government and impose a capitalist system similar to the bipartisan U.S. model. Accordingly, it proposed acting in six areas: promote dissidence; intensify the illegal broadcasts of Radio and TV Martí to Cuba; strangle the Cuban economy; create propaganda about the supposed military threat posed by Cuba; intensify international campaigns against the Cuban government; and, eventually, occupy the country. The plan was allocated a publicly announced budget of fifty-nine million dollars. In particular, measures were implemented to reduce visits by Cuban Americans to the island and decrease the amount of remittances they sent. The plan presented in the 2006 report created a "Cuba Fund" of eighty million dollars to promote a two-year project of internal subversion and allocated twenty million annually to end the "dictatorship" in Cuba.

Despite this aggressive stance of the Bush government, by 2004, the United States supplied 44 percent of Cuba's agricultural imports,

---

* The U.S. Senate's Church Committee substantiated eight CIA attempts to assassinate Fidel Castro over 1960–1965. Fabian Escalante, a retired chief of Cuba's counterintelligence and tasked with protecting Fidel Castro, estimated 638 CIA assassination schemes or actual attempts.

authorized since 2001. In 2006, the United States provided 96 percent of its rice and 77 percent of its poultry. In 2008 the island's food imports reached eight hundred million dollars and the United States became its fourth-largest trading partner in this important category.

The most aggressive phase of the George W. Bush administrations lasted from June 2002 until August 2006, when there was a language shift by secretary of state Condoleezza Rice and assistant secretary of state for western hemisphere affairs, Thomas Shannon, who returned to the more "conciliatory" tone used by Bush in his speeches in Miami and the White House on May 20, 2002.

In his presidential campaign, Barack Obama (2009–2017) stated that he would eliminate the restrictions that Bush had imposed on remittances for shipping various kinds of goods and would travel to Cuba, indicating his willingness to engage in dialogue with the Cuban government while maintaining the embargo.

At the Summit of the Americas of April 2009, he declared, "I'm prepared to have my administration engage with the Cuban government on a wide range of issues—from drugs, migration, and economic issues, to human rights, free speech, and democratic reform."[24] Raúl Castro also proposed, days before the Summit, his willingness to dialogue with the United States on any issue.

During his first term, Obama liberalized U.S. policy toward Cuba with various measures:

1. He lifted restrictions on sending remittances but requested the Cuban government to reduce the fee (discount rate) it charged on them.
2. He eliminated restrictions on travel by Cuban Americans to Cuba.
3. He broadened the concept of family and therefore increased the number of people eligible to receive remittances.
4. He made the restrictions on both remittances and travel more flexible, which increased the amount of money that Cuban Americans could spend on the island.
5. He authorized negotiation between U.S. telecommunication companies and the Cuban company ETECSA, allowing Cuban Americans residing in the United States to pay for Internet and cell phone service for their relatives in Cuba.
6. He increased the maximum value and expanded the list of articles and products that could be shipped to the island.

However, despite these measures, he supported maintaining the embargo, conditioned dialogue with the island on its complying with U.S. "principles" on human rights and democracy, continued to designate Cuba as a terrorist country, and demanded that Cuba comply with the provisions of the OAS Charter.

Nevertheless, Obama's policy exhibited an essential difference from his predecessor's: it avoided aggressive rhetoric and was more flexible in everything that directly affected the average person, such as travel and remittances. However, it maintained the harshest aspects of the blockade, such as the fines on banks that had business dealings with Cuba. In addition, it continued financing attempts to subvert the revolution through the Internet (ZunZuneo) and other measures.*

On January 10, 2010, minister of foreign relations Bruno Rodríguez Parilla proposed to the U.S. government an agenda of what the Cuban government considered the essential issues that had to be addressed in a process of dialogue and negotiation aimed at improving relations: lifting the economic, trade, and financial blockade; removing Cuba from the list of terrorist states; repealing the Cuban Adjustment Act and the "wet foot–dry foot" policy; compensating Cuba for economic and human damage; returning the territory occupied by the Guantánamo Naval Base; ending radio and television aggression from the United States against Cuba; and ceasing to finance internal subversion. A key issue on this agenda was freedom for the "Cuban Five," who remained imprisoned in the United States, an issue Cubans considered a major injustice. On November 13, 2012, in the UN General Assembly, Foreign Minister Rodríguez Parilla proposed to the United States "to negotiate cooperation agreements in areas of greatest mutual interest, such as combating drug trafficking, terrorism, human trafficking and for the full normalization of migratory relations, as well as for the prevention and mitigation of natural disasters, protection of the environment and our common seas." He also suggested "a resumption of the talks unilaterally suspended by our counterpart about migratory issues and the resumption of postal services."[25]

In 2013, the Obama administration resumed talks with Cuba over specific issues of common interest that had been suspended since 2009,

---

* In April 2014, the Associated Press revealed the existence of the already mythical "Cuban Twitter," known as ZunZuneo, through which the U.S. government intended to use cell phones to push for regime change in Cuba.

following the arrest of USAID contractor Alan Gross, who had tried to create a clandestine Internet in Cuba, as part of Washington's strategy of destabilization.

In May 2014, the assistant secretary of state for the western hemisphere, Roberta Jacobson, and the director of the U.S. section of the Ministry of Foreign Relations of Cuba, Josefina Vidal, met in Washington to initiate ongoing discussions on matters of mutual interest. After negotiations throughout 2014 and a long telephone conversation between the Cuban and U.S. presidents, they agreed to begin the process of restoring diplomatic relations.

On December 17, 2014, Obama announced, "I've instructed Secretary Kerry to immediately begin discussions with Cuba to reestablish diplomatic relations that have been severed since January of 1961."[26] That same day, Cuban president Raúl Castro declared, "We have agreed to renew diplomatic relations."[27]

Once Obama realized that, on the one hand, the transition in Cuba from Fidel to Raúl Castro was not destabilizing the island and, on the other, that there was consensus among the U.S. political elites and in broad sectors of society—including the majority of Cuban Americans—that policy toward the island should change, he decided to initiate the process of reestablishing relations.

NOTES

1. López Segrera, *Cuba: capitalismo dependiente y subdesarrollo*; López Segrera, *Raíces históricas*.

2. F. Castro, "History Will Absolve Me."

3. López Segrera, *Raíces históricas*.

4. Smith, *Closest of Enemies*, 99.

5. López Segrera, *Cuba Cairá?* López Segrera, *Cuba sans l'URSS*; López Segrera, *Cuba después del colapso*; López Segrera, *La Revolución Cubana*.

6. Kennedy, "Opinion: We Have So Much"; Kennedy, "Opinion: JFK's Secret Negotiations"; Kennedy, "Opinion: Sabotaging U.S.-Cuba Détente."

7. Kennedy, "Opinion: JFK's Secret Negotiations."

8. Ibid.

9. Daniel, "Unofficial Envoy."

10. Daniel, "I Was There When Castro Heard the News."

11. Attwood, *Twilight Struggle*, 263.

12. Kennedy, "Opinion: Sabotaging U.S.-Cuba Détente."

13. Attwood, *Twilight Struggle*, 263.
14. F. Castro, "Interview of Fidel Castro."
15. G. H. W. Bush, "Another Perspective."
16. Clinton, "Statement on Cuban Independence Day."
17. F. Castro, "Varadero News Conference."
18. F. Castro, "Comparecencia del presidente Fidel Castro."
19. Clinton, "Preface to the Report."
20. Albright, "U.S. Announces Steps."
21. "Castro Cautiously Welcomes Changes," *Washington Post*.
22. Bolton, "Beyond the Axis of Evil."
23. G. W. Bush, "Remarks on Cuba."
24. Obama, "Remarks by the President."
25. Rodríguez Parrilla, "Speech by Bruno Rodríguez Parrilla."
26. Obama, "Statement by the President."
27. R. Castro, "Presidential Letter to Obama."

Chapter Two

Mutual Perceptions (1959–2015)

As the Cuban Revolution advanced, Cuba and the United States viewed their relations from very different perspectives.

CUBA'S FOREIGN POLICY (1959–2015)

Cuba's foreign policy evolved in response to both national and international developments including the fall of the Soviet Union and the political correlation of forces in Latin America and the third world.

Primary Periods

Chapter 1 presented the primary periods of the Cuban Revolution. This chapter will formulate a periodization of Cuba's international relations and its foreign policy.

The principal characteristics of the different periods are as follows:

1959–1962

U.S. policy caused Cuba to perceive the United States as an aggressive power that threatened its national sovereignty and tried to prevent the changes necessary to transform its neocolonial status.

1962–1970

The Cuban Revolution was isolated due to the U.S. blockade. The Vietnam War and the U.S.-Soviet agreements in 1962 contributed to the U.S. government abandoning new aggressive military projects, such as the failed Bay of Pigs invasion of Cuba in 1961.

After a period (**1965–1968**) of active Cuban support for national liberation movements and Che Guevara's death in Bolivia,* a new phase was characterized by better relations with the Soviet Union; a low-profile policy toward national liberation movements; an increase in Cuba's international action in the third world through bilateral agreements; a more active presence in the United Nations and in the Non-Aligned Movement (NAM); and the restoration of ties with Latin America and the Caribbean at the end of the 1960s and beginning of the 1970s.

1970–1979

The most important developments in this period were the weakening of the U.S. blockade at the global level and especially in Latin America and the Caribbean (LAC), the new prominence of Cuba in other international arenas through agreements of various kinds; growing diplomatic relations with LAC; Cuba's entry into the Council for Mutual Economic Cooperation (COMECON) in 1972; some improvement in its relations with the United States; the expansion of international assistance to developing countries in areas such as medicine, education, construction, and military affairs; the creation of the Latin American Economic System (SELA) in 1975 that excluded the United States; and the celebration in Havana of the VI Summit of the NAM in 1979.

Cuba's prestige and influence in the third world reached its highest point at the meetings of the NAM in Algiers (1973)—where it was elected to the presidency—and in Havana (1979), and as a result of its military victories in Angola, against apartheid, and in Ethiopia. We can add the success of the revolutions in Nicaragua and Grenada in 1979 and the restoration of diplomatic relations with Anglophone Caribbean countries. Ties with the Soviet Union were strengthened, significantly enhancing harmonious foreign relations with that country,

---

* Che Guevara departed for Bolivia in 1966, where he attempted to create a guerrilla force that would lead a revolutionary struggle in the heart of South America. He was captured and executed by a CIA-backed Bolivian army unit in 1967.

which—along with Cuba's leadership in the third world—created a crisis for U.S. hegemony in the United Nations and other international organizations.

1979–1989

During this period, Cuba consolidated its relations with the majority of the world's nations. In 1988, the island had diplomatic relations with 125 countries. Of these, seventy had embassies in Havana while Cuba had eighty-nine diplomatic missions abroad. During the ultraconservative Reagan (1981–1989) and George H. W. Bush (1989–1993) administrations, relations with the United States entered a more difficult period, given the increased hostility of these Republican governments toward the island.

Cuba's role in the NAM presidency weakened after the Soviet invasion of Afghanistan in 1979, which was condemned by numerous nonaligned countries. Cuba tried to create a movement opposed to the increase in foreign debt, but the governments of the third world, especially those of LAC, preferred to negotiate their debts bilaterally and avoid confrontation with their creditors.

During this period, Cuba suffered setbacks in foreign policy in LAC when Jamaica, Grenada, Suriname, Costa Rica, Colombia, and Venezuela broke diplomatic relations. However, this was offset by the restoration of relations with Bolivia, Uruguay, Brazil, and Argentina, as well as the normalization of relations with Ecuador and Peru in 1984 and 1986.

1989–2015

From the fall of the Soviet Union and the socialist countries in Europe to the restoration of Cuban-U.S. diplomatic relations, the emergence of the United States as a world hegemonic power posed a serious threat to Cuba in this period. However, the reinforcement of multipolar spaces in Asia, the Arab countries, Africa, and Europe provided room to maneuver and the possibility of alternative alliances in the international arena. The trilateral relationship of the United States, Europe, and Japan facilitated the emergence of an increasingly multipolar world represented by China, India, Russia, Brazil, Iran, South Africa, and Venezuela. This has offered Cuba, in addition to its traditional relations with LAC, the European Union, and Canada, a new arena for its international relations despite the disappearance of "actually existing socialism." Today the island has diplomatic relations with 178 countries, almost four times more than when the revolution came to power in 1959.

The principal directions of the Cuban Revolution's foreign policy were developed in the speeches of Fidel and Raúl Castro and institutionalized in key documents such as the First (1961) and Second (1962) Declaration of Havana and in the documents of the Congresses of the Communist Party of Cuba (PCC). Its principles have been internationalism and the struggle to achieve peace and survive the aggressive policy of U.S. governments.

From the Cuban perspective, in contrast to the United States, Cuba has successfully met the objectives and followed the principles of its foreign policy: surviving U.S. attacks and lending its solidarity and aid to liberation movements of various kinds.

Just as U.S. policy toward its Cuban neocolony made necessary a revolution as profound as Cuba's, demonstrating that policy's total failure, U.S. policy toward the Cuban revolutionary process from 1959 until the present has brought about exactly the opposite of what it sought.

The United States intended to destroy the Cuban Revolution with the blockade and began efforts to subvert it, leading a broad group of Latin American governments in this endeavor. The results were an increasingly close relationship between Cuba and the Soviet Union, which provided resources for development that the United States had denied and also Cuban support, in legitimate self-defense, for revolutionaries in the countries allied with Washington in its anti-Cuba campaign. This in no way means that Cuba has constructed a socialist revolution or that it has supported internationalism merely as a defensive reaction. But what Cubans emphasize is that U.S. policy did not leave Cuba any alternative other than a confrontation that it never sought.

On the other hand, the bitterness of the Cuban-U.S. conflict is due not just to a U.S. political line that resists renouncing neocolonial paternalism. It also reflects the ideological obsession of the Eisenhower and Bush administrations and, most of all, the crisis affecting the traditional structures of U.S. domination in its "backyard" since the end of the 1960s that have now been eliminated not only in Cuba but also in another group of countries in the region—Venezuela, Ecuador, Bolivia, Nicaragua, Argentina, Brazil, and Uruguay. These structures are also in crisis and threatened with being swept away in other countries where U.S. domination has polarized these societies between an elite at the service of Washington and the broad impoverished masses. Despite the fall of the Soviet Union and Eastern Europe, the growing multipolarity of the current global order has involved the emergence of political spaces favorable for Cuba in the region and at the global level. Resounding failures of U.S. policy toward the region have been the Alliance for Progress, recommendations of the Kissinger Report, the Caribbean Basin Initiative, and the defeat of the Free Trade Area of the Americas (FTAA) in Mar del Plata (2005).

U.S. policy toward Cuba has not achieved its objectives. Cuba plays an important leadership role in the Non-Aligned Movement; it maintained close relations with the countries of COMECON until its dissolution in 1989; and it maintains close relations with the Latin American and Caribbean countries associated with CELAC (Community of Latin American and Caribbean States) and ALBA (Bolivarian Alliance for the Peoples of Our America), with BRICS (Brazil, Russia, India, China, and South Africa), with developed capitalist countries, and with third world nations, to which it extends solidarity and aid.

Cuba's International Relations in a Multipolar World Order

The world order's increasing multipolarity favors the changes underway in Cuba. Similar to the "updating of the economic model" that the Cuban government is implementing, its foreign policy is being reformulated to be realistic, pragmatic, more discreet, and less visible.[1]

Cuba's long-term support for colonial and neocolonial struggles and its various kinds of collaboration with countries of the third world have given it considerable political capital.

The process culminating in the reestablishment of diplomatic relations with the United States took place in a context of the progressive expansion of Cuba's international relations. Although Cuba's leading role is more evident in Latin America and the Caribbean, its current relations with BRICS—especially with their most relevant actors, Russia and China—form part of this process. The beginning of negotiations with the European Union for the establishment of a Political Dialogue and Cooperation Agreement is another clear step in that direction.

The emergence of postneoliberal governments in the region, on one hand, and the high degree of autonomy of the region as a whole, on the other, achieved in forums such as CELAC—whose Second Summit was held in Havana in January 2014 without the presence of actors from outside the region—have contributed to strengthening the key role of the island in Latin America and the Caribbean through regional and bilateral cooperation.

The presence of leftist governments that are developing alternatives to neoliberalism in the region has involved a strengthening of Cuba's relations with these countries, including Venezuela, Nicaragua, Ecuador, Bolivia, Brazil, Argentina, Uruguay, and El Salvador.

Cuba's exclusion from the Organization of American States (OAS)—until the Panama summit in April 2015—and the FTAA does not mean that it is isolated in the region. The most important multilateral regional agreements to which Cuba belongs are CELAC, ALBA, Petrocaribe, the Latin American Association of Integration (ALADI), SELA, the Association of Caribbean States, and the Bank of the South. In addition, Cuba has agreements of association with institutions such as Caricom and Mercosur, without being a formal member.

Its main bilateral agreements in the region are with Venezuela, with which it exchanges the work of health and other professionals for oil, and with Brazil to develop a variety of projects, especially the container terminal and Mariel Special Development Zone, a project that contributes to Cuba's insertion into international production and trade chains. It also encourages foreign investment, especially in areas such as the pharmaceutical, auto, packaging, and other industries.

China and Russia are two strategic allies of Cuba, and in July 2014, the presidents of both countries, Xi Jiping and Vladimir Putin, visited the island.

China is Cuba's second-largest trade partner after Venezuela. It has extended various lines of commercial credit and is contributing to the development of oil exploration and production on the island. There are important similarities with China in regard to the construction of a socialist market economy and the one-party character of the institutions of both countries.

Russia's forgiveness of 90 percent of Cuba's debt led to greater collaboration in all areas. During Vladimir Putin's visit to Havana, ten agreements were signed including a particularly significant one for oil exploration. Moreover, the Cuban armed forces use Russian weapons, strengthening relations in the military and security field.

Cuba continues to strengthen its relations with the U.S. allies Canada, the European Union, and Japan. The collaboration with Canada has always been especially important for the island, and good relations with its government have been maintained over the years despite some difficult moments. Canada is Cuba's main source of tourism and its third-largest trading partner. It is second in the importance and breadth of its investments and in the volume of official cooperation with Cuba. Especially important is the role of Sheritt International, the multinational mining company, which in the 1990s focused on the nickel industry but recently has expanded into tourism and oil.[2] Canada, in cooperation with the Vatican, played a key role in facilitating early steps in the process of reestablishing Cuban-U.S. diplomatic relations.

Relations with the European Union began improving in 2008. Since they were established in 1989, relations between Brussels and Havana have gone through difficult times. They were adversely affected by the adoption of the Common Position in 1996 and the sanctions the European Union agreed to in 2003. Despite this, the European Union is the island's second-largest trading partner, its main source of direct foreign investment and cooperation for development, and its third-largest tourism client. In the bilateral sphere, eighteen cooperation agreements have been signed along with a similar number for the promotion and protection of investments with EU member countries. European companies such as Pernod Ricard, Sol Melia, and Castrol, among others, operate in Cuba. Recently, both sides have begun talks on a Political Dialogue and Cooperation Agreement.

Cuba has always given great importance to its relations with developing countries in a framework of international solidarity. In the Middle East, Cuba will continue to support the Palestinian cause and to strengthen its relations with countries in the area. Cuba will also maintain an important presence in Africa, cooperating in civilian fields such as health and education, although not in military terms and with less visibility than in the 1970s and 1980s. The African roots of Cuban culture and the prestige it enjoys in Africa are elements that will contribute to Cuba's maintaining strong relations with the African states and peoples.

Cuba's role in the Non-Aligned Movement, its independence and sovereignty, and its international solidarity and cooperation in many areas, especially in public health, have contributed to increasing its influence and prestige. Cuban doctors and health professionals are present all over the world, from South Africa to the Pacific Islands, including countries of the Middle East, such as Qatar. The role of Cuban health personnel in Haiti's earthquake and in the fight against Ebola in Africa is internationally recognized. Its relations with Vietnam, Angola, and Iran also merit special mention, because in addition to their economic weight, they contribute to the diversification of Cuba's trade relations.

Cuba's third world leadership and desire to establish a new world order based on peace agreements will continue to sustain its international relevance. The following sections will summarize the factors most relevant in Cuba's international relations during the last decades.

The main accusations of various U.S. administrations (Eisenhower, Kennedy, Johnson, Nixon, Ford, Carter, Reagan, and G. H. W. Bush) against the Cuban Revolution have been based on its relations with the Soviet Union and its support for national liberation movements. After the fall of the Soviet Union, the new preconditions set by Clinton, G. W. Bush, and Obama for recognizing the island's government and lifting the blockade were the need to establish a Western-style democracy in Cuba and respect human rights, demands that the Carter administration had added to the two earlier arguments.

In the 1990s, the United States passed two laws with extraterritorial effects to reinforce the blockade: the Torricelli (1992) and Helms-Burton (1996) acts. However, neither of these laws succeeded in isolating Cuba, although they did damage the country in several ways. In the last few years, only the United States, Israel, and another less prominent international actor have voted against lifting the blockade in the UN General Assembly. This trend of voting against the blockade has grown stronger over time and has isolated the United States rather than Cuba.

In 1996, the European Union adopted a policy called "the Common Position" toward the island, promoted by the José Aznar presidency in Spain. This involved the subordination of Europe's policy to the hostile U.S. policy toward Cuba.

Cuba's relation with Venezuela and ALBA member countries; its deepening relations with Brazil and the Mercosur countries, as well as its strong relations with China, Russia, and various Arab and African countries; its traditional relations with Spain and developed capitalist countries; and its relations with Canada and the Vatican—both of which played a key role in the process of restoring Cuban-U.S. diplomatic relations—contribute to the island's solid standing in the international arena. Even countries that are rhetorically critical of Cuba, such as some in Europe, have important trade relations and investments on the island. Since 2008, relations with the European Union have been gradually improving, a process that accelerated following announcement of the plans to reestablish diplomatic relations.

Cuba's example has served to motivate other countries struggling against dependency and underdevelopment. And above all, it has succeeded in preserving its revolution despite the U.S. eagerness for its destruction.

DIFFERENT PERCEPTIONS OF THE CONFLICT

The U.S. view of the Cuban Revolution arises from its understanding of U.S.-Cuban relations dating from the nineteenth-century and the Cuban struggle for independence from Spain. Examining this historical context reveals the importance of the cultural frames and categories that shape how events are perceived.

The Legitimation of Domination in the U.S. Imagination

For U.S. economic and political elites, Cuba was destined to satisfy U.S. needs and serve U.S. interests. Cuba—and the Cuban people—was a means to that end. The United States came to perceive and "know" Cuba mainly through representations that were completely of its own creation. The Cuba that the U.S. population chose to relate to was, in fact, a product of its own imagination and a projection of its needs. Americans rarely dealt with Cuban reality on its own terms, accepting its internal logic; with Cubans as a people with their own history; or with Cuba as a nation with its own destiny.* It has always been that way from president Thomas Jefferson (1801–1809) to George W. Bush (2001–2009). It appears that this vision and perception has begun to change with Barack Obama.

U.S. expansionism in the nineteenth century took the well-known form of acquisition of the colonial possessions of Spain and France in North America and seizure of a huge amount of Mexico's territory. Already by November 1805 President Thomas Jefferson (1801–1809)

---

* A detailed analysis is found in L. A. Pérez, *Cuba in the American Imagination.*

had informed England's diplomatic representative in the United States that in case of war with Spain, it would take over Cuba.

John Quincy Adams, President James Monroe's (1817–1825) secretary of state who succeeded him as president, formulated the theory of ripe fruit in an April 23, 1923, memorandum: "There are laws of political as well as physical gravitation; and if an apple severed by its native tree cannot choose but fall to the ground, Cuba, forcibly disjoined from its own unnatural connection with Spain, and incapable of self-support, can gravitate only towards the North American Union which by the same law of nature, cannot cast her off its bosom."[3] President Monroe, on December 2, 1823, formulated the Monroe Doctrine, stating that the United States would consider "any attempt" on the part of European powers "to extend their system to any portion of this hemisphere as dangerous to our peace and safety."[4]

All U.S. presidents and secretaries of state since Monroe and Adams pursued the following policy toward Cuba as a Spanish colony: avoiding any commitment that involved giving up the goal of ruling the island, opposing attempts by other powers and of Cubans to promote Cuba's independence, and offering to buy the island from Spain. President William McKinley (1897–1901), consistent with these aims, intervened in 1898 in the Cuban war for independence from Spain, which the Cubans had almost won and, with the help of Theodore Roosevelt (1901–1909), imposed the neocolonial model that prevailed until 1959.

Cubans' efforts to free themselves from Spanish colonialism were frustrated in three successive wars: the Ten Years' War (1869–1878), the Little War (1879–1880), and the War of Independence (1895–1898).

The politically dominant U.S. elites successfully created and disseminated an ideology based on metaphors to justify the aspirations to annex Cuba and legitimize intervention in the war of 1898. Therefore it is important to analyze the use of metaphor and its role in political discourse.

Starting in the sixteenth century, Cuba's significance was constructed using colonial metaphors such as the "Key to the New World" and the "Key to the Gulf," as a symbol of its position between the two Americas.

Metaphor was also used in the nineteenth century to persuade U.S. citizens that possessing Cuba was indispensable to future U.S. well-being and a matter of national necessity. Having fulfilled the Manifest Destiny of expanding from the Atlantic to the Pacific Coast and having taken possession of almost a third of Mexico's territory, it was time to seize the ripe fruit.*

Since Cuba penetrated the U.S. imagination through metaphors that justified U.S. policies and interests to the general public, what were the main metaphors that helped legitimate U.S. plans for imperial domination of Cuba?

As already mentioned, John Quincy Adams visualized the island as subject to the law of gravity that would cause it to fall into the U.S. lap as "ripe fruit."[5] Another metaphor presented Cuba as a child to be cared for because of the incompetence of Cubans to govern themselves. The metaphor of the good neighbor highlighted concern about a people abused by Spain; to prevent the continued suffering of Cubans, the United States, like the Good Samaritan, had to intervene in the war against Spain and take over Cuba, which was envisioned as a defenseless, raped woman.

For John Quincy Adams, the annexation of Cuba was "indispensable to the continuance and integrity of the Union itself."[6] Similarly, President James Buchanan (1857–1861) asserted that "we must have Cuba. We can't do without Cuba."[7] The Ostend Manifesto (1854), which advocated the purchase of Cuba from Spain, declared,

> Indeed the Union can never enjoy repose, nor possess reliable security, as long as Cuba is not embraced within its boundaries. . . . The intercourse which its proximity to our coasts begets and encourages between them and the citizens of the United States has, in the progress of time, so united their interests and blended their fortunes that they now look upon each other as if they were one people and had but one destiny.[8]

President Martin Van Buren (1837–1841) explained the United States' "deepest interest" in Cuba because it lies "almost in sight of our southern shores."[9] Even the poet Walt Whitman stated, "Judging from . . . the geographic position of Cuba . . . there can be little doubt that . . . it will gradually be absorbed into the Union. . . . It is impossible to say what the future will bring forth but 'manifest destiny' points to the speedy annexation of Cuba by the United States."[10]

---

* The thesis of Manifest Destiny was developed by the journalist John L. O'Sullivan, who asserted "manifest destiny to overspread and to possess the whole of the continent" in an influential article in *New York Morning News*, December 27, 1845, among other writings popularizing the concept. See "John L. O'Sullivan," *Wikipedia*.

The metaphor based on geographic location led to another that draws a parallel to the physical law of gravity: "the natural, God's law forces [Cuba] to gravitate to the United States," asserted the U.S. general consul in Havana.[11]

A third metaphor was that of the good neighbor worried about the destiny of its close neighbor. President Ulysses Grant (1869–1877) stated that the Ten Years' War was a "protracted struggle in such close proximity to our own territory" that it constituted a reason to intervene in the conflict "in the interest of a neighboring people."[12] During the Ten Years' War, the Committee on Foreign Affairs of the House of Representatives took the position that "the immediate proximity of Cuba to the United States gives to these grave events an importance which cannot be fully appreciated by any other state. . . . The Cuban question becomes, therefore, an American question."[13]

The possible abolition of slavery in Cuba was also a concern, since the example of what happened on the neighboring island was perceived as a threat to domestic peace and the Union's existence.[14]

A fourth metaphor involved Cubans' incompetence in governing themselves. John Quincy Adams described Cubans as "not competent to a system of self-dependence."[15] Louisiana senator Judah Benjamin stated in 1859, "This unfortunate Hispano-American race is incompetent to self-government. Wherever they have tried it, they have had revolution, strife, and civil disorders. The people do not know how to yield to the will of the majority."[16]

This widespread U.S. view of Cuba as a country whose people were incompetent at self-government was reinforced by the specter of Haiti, ruined after its independence. Cuba might become another Haiti, altering the "neighborhood" not only for themselves but also for the region, and thus affecting U.S. economic and commercial interests.

The United States unsuccessfully tried to buy the island, always thinking that the only alternative to Spanish domination was U.S. domination. President Cleveland (1885–1889) considered buying the island, but not granting Cubans independence, since "it would seem absurd for us to buy the island and present it to the people now inhabiting it, and put its government and management in their hands."[17] The *New York Times* explained in April 1898 that war against Spain was coming: "We go to war with Spain not for the accomplishment of an ambition, but in obedience to the laws of nature. It is time this thing were done and we do it, as the ripened fruit drops from the tree."[18]

A fifth metaphor linked that of the good neighbor to the indignation caused by the death of innocent civilians. "We are going to war with Spain," explained Wisconsin senator John Colt Spooner in April 1898 because "we can not any longer listen to the cries, which come floating over the sea upon every breeze from Cuba."[19] The *Washington Evening Star* urged the intervention since "their cries and appeals are distinctly heard in every section of this country."[20] They also claimed that they sensed the aroma of insurrection in Cuba as a stench that had to be eliminated. Song lyrics purported to give voice to the pleas and sobs supposedly heard in the voice of Cuba crying out for U.S. intervention.

Another metaphor compared the massacre of two hundred thousand Armenians by the Ottoman Turks to the situation in Cuba, meaning that the United States could not duplicate Europe's failure to get involved and remain indifferent. This metaphor forced it to act for the same reasons that Americans had demanded European intervention.

The plight of homelessness and the excesses committed by the Spanish soldiers against women and defenseless children sparked outrage in the United States. The use of "reconcentration camps" ordered as of February 16, 1896, by the governor general of the island, Valeriano Weyler, where civilian peasant families were relocated into settlements under military control, caused human losses totaling some three hundred thousand people. These images were used to justify and strengthen interventionist arguments.

A sixth metaphor emerged, of Cuba imagined as a woman victim of Spanish villainy, raped and defenseless, begging for U.S. intervention to save her. The images of the defenseless woman and of children dying of starvation before their mothers' eyes because of Weyler's reconcentration policy was too much. The United States had to rescue the Cuban people.

However, the nature of the neocolonial regime imposed by the U.S. intervention was clear in this letter from the island's military governor, Leonard Wood (1899–1901), to President Theodore Roosevelt:

> There is, of course, little or no independence left Cuba under the Platt Amendment . . . and the only consistent thing to do now is to seek annexation. This, however, will take some time, and during the period [in] which Cuba maintains her own government, it is most desirable that she should be able to maintain such a one as will tend to her betterment and advancement. She can not make certain treaties without our consent, borrow money beyond certain limits and must maintain certain sanitary conditions, etc. from

all of it is quite apparent that she is absolutely in our hands, and I believe that no European government for a moment considers that she is otherwise than a true dependency of the United States and as such is certainly worthy of our consideration. . . . With the control we have over Cuba, a control which soon undoubtedly will become possession, . . . we shall soon practically control the sugar trade of the world. . . . I believe Cuba to be a most desirable acquisition for the United States. The island will . . . gradually become americanized . . . and we shall have in time one of the richest and desirable possessions in the world.[21]

The Republic of Cuba was born under these conditions in 1902. The U.S. intervention in 1898 aborted a struggle for independence that was on the verge of success since the Cuban Liberation Army had almost defeated Spain. This intervention flowed from the U.S. imperialist dynamic. However, the ideological metaphors, which masked its imperial intentions, portrayed the military intervention as putting into practice a laudable humanitarian principle. In the U.S. imagination, the intervention should appear to be and be understood as a moral act. In reality, it ushered in a new era, since it meant the beginning of the imperialist phase of monopoly capitalism, the launch of a model of neocolonial domination that allowed the United States to annex Puerto Rico and the Philippines. Cuba would have to continue to struggle to finally achieve its true, second independence in 1959.

In 1905 Elihu Root, U.S. secretary of state, wrote, "The South Americans now hate us, largely because they think we despise them and want to bully them."[22] Between 1900 and 1925, the United States militarily intervened in Latin America and the Caribbean on numerous occasions: Honduras (1903, 1907, 1911, 1912, 1919, 1924, and 1925); Cuba (1906, 1912, and 1917); Nicaragua (1907, 1910, and 1912); Dominican Republic (1903, 1914, and 1916); Haiti (1914); Panama (1908, 1912, 1918, 1921, and 1925); Mexico (1914); and Guatemala (1920).

The U.S. magazine the *Nation* critiqued this interventionism on June 7, 1922:

There are, or were, twenty independent republics to the south of us. Five at least—Cuba, Panama, Haiti, Santo Domingo and Nicaragua—have already been reduced to the status of colonies with at most a degree of rather fictitious self-government. Four more—Guatemala, Honduras, Costa Rica and Peru—appear to be in the process of reduction to the same status. . . . How far is this to go? Is the United States to create . . . an empire ruled by a group of Wall Street bankers at whose disposal the State and the Navy Departments graciously place their resources?[23]

Differing Cuban and U.S. Perceptions

In contrast to the U.S. understandings described in the previous section, the Cuban perception is synthesized in this letter that José Martí, leader of the war for independence, wrote on May 18, 1985, from the Dos Rios encampment, to his friend, Manuel Mercado: "Every-day now I am in danger of giving my life for my country and duty—since I understand it and have the spirit to carry it out—in order to prevent, by the timely independence of Cuba, the United States from extending its hold across the Antilles and falling with all the greater force on the lands of our America. All I have done up to now and all I will do is for that."[24]

After the birth of the republic in 1902 the perceptions of the two actors continued to be totally different. Between 1902 and 1959 Cuban nationalists viewed the United States as an interventionist country that had imposed dependence on Cuba. For the United States, Cuba was a sugar reserve and a market for its manufactured products. Cubans found themselves faced with the contradiction that any nationalist demand would lead to U.S. intervention. The United States worried that the neocolonial relationship could lead to a revolution, and in that case—after a U.S.-imposed blockade—Cuba would become integrated into the Soviet market, just as had been predicted in a 1935 Foreign Policy Association report.[25]

The neocolonial relationship was in the interest of the Cuban political class and the oligarchic, antinational Cuban-U.S.-Spanish bloc and its clients because in the U.S. market they benefited from the preferential prices the United States established for the sugar quota. For the governments in Washington, Cuba represented a secure supply of sugar in case of war—as occurred during World War I, World War II, and the Korean War—a nearby market for its products, and a source of dividends from the more than one billion dollars that U.S. capital had invested in the island.

However, the neocolonial model, despite its "advantages," by excluding increasingly important sectors of Cuban society while simultaneously offending creole nationalism with the Platt Amendment and its consequences and supporting the dictator Batista, generated its opposite: the Cuban Revolution.

Once it realized that the defeat of Batista was imminent, the United States tried to snatch the revolutionary triumph away from Fidel Castro and the forces he headed, attempting to achieve a "government without Castro." Fidel had already predicted this outcome in a June 5, 1958, letter from the Sierra Maestra to Celia Sanchez, a close colleague and leader of the 26th of July Movement, when he wrote, "Seeing the rockets they fired at Mario's house, I swore that the Americans are going to pay dearly for what they are doing. When this war is over, a much longer and greater war will start for me: the war I will wage against them. I realize that this is going to be my true destiny."[26]

The analysis of U.S. policy toward Cuba in specific periods allows us to identify the perceptions of both countries, the contradictions, interests, mutual advantages, and disadvantages that would come from the resolution of the conflict, and possible negotiation scenarios and policy alternatives.

1959–1962: From the Victory of the Revolution to the Nuclear Missile Crisis

Since 1958, and especially since 1959, the revolution's leadership perceived the United States as an aggressive power that intended to undermine Cuba's sovereignty and prevent changes to the neocolonial order.

The Cuban leadership, to be faithful to its program and satisfy the aspirations and needs of the revolution's new social subjects, inevitably had to affect the neocolonial order and, therefore, U.S. interests in Cuba.

The contradictions with the United States tended to increase during the first period of the Cuban Revolution (1959–1962). In Cuba's view, the U.S. government had attacked it economically (embargo/blockade); politically (breaking diplomatic relations, supporting the counterrevolution, and not recognizing Fidel's leadership); militarily (Bay of Pigs invasion and October missile crisis of 1962); and internationally (expulsion from the OAS) with the aim of destroying the revolution and showing the nonviability of the Cuban project to other Latin American countries, among other objectives. The United States used the metaphor of "the revolution betrayed" by its own leaders to legitimate its aggressive policy.

Cuba was left with only one alternative—just as the analysts of the Foreign Policy Association had predicted in 1935—integration into the socialist, and especially Soviet, market. It moved in this direction by re-

establishing relations with the Soviet Union on May 8, 1960, as already
noted, and with China in September of that year. In the international
arena, it fought against the U.S. attempt to isolate it by participating in
founding the Non-Aligned Movement in 1961—which it also joined out
of principle and by meeting the essential requirement of not belonging
to any military pact—and by broadening and strengthening its relations,
not only with European and Asian socialist countries but also with capitalist countries that were not subservient to Washington.

In this period, the United States viewed the island as a Soviet ally (especially after May 1960 when Cuban-Soviet relations were established)
that constituted a threat to its national security and the U.S. order in
Latin America and the Caribbean.

At this stage, it also perceived Cuba as a country led by a political
class that was dismantling the neocolonial order. Acknowledging that
the Cuban project implied legitimating social change that affected the
United States politically (it did not control the new political leadership as in the past); economically (the revolution's development plans
inevitably affected concentrated land ownership, industrial and market
monopolies, U.S. investments, and the entire structure imposed by
Washington since 1902); and militarily (the U.S. military mission that
had advised the Batista dictatorship was sent home, the Cuban army
would no longer be an extension of U.S. forces that could be used in
wars like Korea, and Cuba might threaten the United States, given its
alliance with the Soviet Union).

The alternative to its aggressive policy was for Washington to accept the new Cuban reality, seek new mutually beneficial links within
the new framework, and accept an adequate compensation for the na-
tionalization of its properties, as did Switzerland, Canada, Spain, and
the United Kingdom, among others. Instead the United States chose
to promote subversion against the Cuban government, isolate it internationally, and try to prevent the country's economic development.
According to the testimony of Wayne Smith, a U.S. embassy official in
Cuba during that period, Washington pursued two essential objectives,
among others, supporting the internal opposition and working with the
OAS to put a "*cordon sanitaire* around Cuba," to prevent its example
from spreading to other countries in the region.[27]

The period concluded with the October Crisis of 1962, also known as
the Cuban Missile Crisis. The way the crisis was managed represents a
lost opportunity. The United States and the Soviet Union agreed that if

the Soviet Union would withdraw its missiles from Cuba under UN su-
pervision, the United States would lift the naval blockade of the island
and make a commitment not to invade it. However, Cuba was excluded
from the negotiations by both the United States and the Soviet Union
and as a result did not allow the UN inspection. A different *modus vi-
vendi* between Cuba and the United States could have been created that
was more in accord with the island's legitimate interests—expressed in
a five-point statement of the Cuban position—and based on a relationship among equals that respected Cuban sovereignty.*

1962–1970: From the Missile Crisis to Breaking Out of International Isolation

Although during the 1962–1970 period the Cuban-U.S. conflict tended
to adopt less intense forms, Cuba continued to view Washington as a
hostile power—engaged in the economic blockade, other campaigns
against Cuba, sabotage, promotion of counterrevolutionary groups,
and other operations of this kind—and as a world policeman waging
the Vietnam War. In testimony before the Senate Foreign Relations
Committee, U.S. secretary of state Dean Rusk pointed out that the
objectives of the blockade on Cuba were "to reduce Castro's will and
ability to export subversion and violence to other American states; to
make it plain to the people of Cuba that Castro's regime cannot serve
their interests; to demonstrate to the people of the American Republics
that communism has no future in the Western Hemisphere; to increase
the cost to the Soviet Union of maintaining a communist outpost in the
Western Hemisphere."[28]

In terms of policy making and implementation, after a period of
support for national liberation movements, which reached its height
between 1967 and 1968, Cuba tended to modify its policies in several
directions: notably, improving its relationship with the Soviet Union; in

---

* Fidel, finding the terms under which the missile crisis was resolved to be unsatisfactory,
issued a declaration on October 28 that was sent to UN secretary general U. Thant, in which
he proposed the following: (1) End the economic blockade and all U.S. measures to apply
commercial and economic pressure against Cuba all over the world. (2) End all subversive
activities—launching and deployment of arms and explosives by air and sea, organizing invasions by mercenaries, infiltration by spies, and acts of sabotage—all carried out from U.S. territory and from some accomplice countries. (3) Cease pirate attacks carried out from existing
bases in the United States and Puerto Rico. (4) Cease all violations of air and sea space by
U.S. warplanes and ships. (5) Withdraw from the Guantánamo naval base and return Cuban
territory occupied by the United States ("Document 56").

the third world increasingly acting though official channels; in a variety of other ways and through the NAM; and initiating rapprochement with governments in Latin America and the Caribbean.

From 1962 to 1970, the United States saw Cuba as an increasingly strong ally of the Soviet Union—especially after 1968—and as an exporter of revolution, at least until the end of the period. The United States developed the Alliance for Progress and counterinsurgency as a political-military doctrine to confront the Cuban Revolution in Latin America and the Caribbean and national liberation movements in general. It adopted covert paramilitary actions against Cuba (known as Operation Mongoose) but tended to moderate some of its positions toward the end of the period.

1970–1979: From Cuba's International Leadership to the Carter Administration's Ambivalence

Between 1970 and 1979 Cuba perceived the United States as an aggressive power that had been defeated in Vietnam and was experiencing a crisis of hegemony. The show of force by the third world via the formation of OPEC in 1973 emphasized what Cuba viewed as the weakness of Western developed capitalism. During this phase, the leadership of the revolution, seeing a favorable attitude in sectors of the U.S. political class, reanalyzed the advantages that reestablishing relations with the United States would bring: elimination of the blockade, recovery of the Guantánamo base and the end of aggression; possibilities of trade in sugar, rum, nickel, rice, corn, fertilizer, machinery, and other products; a nearby market that would reduce costs for shipping and warehousing; access to capitalist markets (their technology and credit); and reduction of tensions that would allow decreasing military spending and therefore speed up development. This would involve U.S. acknowledgment of Cuba's equality in the international arena and could even mean granting it most-favored-nation status on the same terms as other LAC countries not subjected to a blockade.

The gradual rapprochement and possible restoration of relations could also present challenges for Cuba. It could erode the values of the development model based on austerity that prioritizes the ideological struggle. It could also prevent the correction of internal errors in the process of building socialism by assigning responsibility for problems in economic performance to the blockade.

Although Cuba took important steps toward the resolution of the conflict with the United States during this stage, it maintained its active and radical nonaligned and internationalist policy.

In Latin America and the Caribbean during this period, Cuba extended its international presence, reestablishing relations with many countries. The improvement of Cuba's relations with the United States and with LAC helped to improve its relations on a worldwide scale with Western Europe, Japan, Canada, and other countries.*

Throughout the 1970s, in the context of détente with the Soviet Union, the United States tended to be less reluctant to reestablish relations with Cuba. The change in Cuba's policy in Latin America and the Caribbean contributed to this, as did its reestablishment of relations with various countries in the region. Nevertheless, at the end of the decade, the perception changed. Neoconservative thinking contributed to disseminating an image of Cuba as a Soviet ally that promoted subversion in Africa, Latin America, and the Caribbean, unconcerned about whether these actions were detrimental to improving its relations with the United States.† According to this interpretation—which became dominant when it was adopted by national security advisor Zbigniew Brzezinski in the final years of the Carter presidency—U.S. "concessions" had only emboldened Cuba.

Prior to the imposition of Reagan's "new vision"—formulated by intellectuals from *Commentary* magazine such as Norman Podhoretz and Constantine Menges and expressed in the First and Second Santa Fe Documents‡—between 1977 and 1978 various delegations of U.S.

---

* In 1975, with the United States voting in favor, Brazil and Nicaragua abstaining, and only Chile, Paraguay, and Uruguay opposed, the majority of OAS countries voted to lift the collective sanctions that the organization had applied to Cuba in 1964, giving member countries freedom to "normalize or conduct in accordance with national policy and interests of each their relations with the Republic of Cuba at the level and in the form that each state deems advisable." Binder, "Cuba Sanctions."

† In reality, the United States used Cuba's military involvement in Angola and Ethiopia—and some of its other foreign policy actions—as pretexts for not fully restoring diplomatic relations, according to Wayne Smith, chief of mission of the U.S. Interests Section in Havana during the Carter administration, sources cited in his book, and others. On the other hand, the idea that full restoration of relations could be achieved step by step—a policy of normalization advocated by authors such as Smith and William LeoGrande and intellectual and political sectors generally linked to the Democrat Party and the Carter administration—did not become widely accepted because the United States lacked the political will to do so. See Smith, *Closest of Enemies*, 94, 104, 117.

‡ These reports were produced by the Committee of Santa Fe, affiliated with the conservative Council for Inter-American Security. The first report, officially titled *A New Inter-American Policy for the Eighties*, appeared in 1980 and was more influential than *Santa Fe II*, which was not published until 1988, near the end of the Reagan presidency.

businessmen visited Cuba, representing more than two hundred companies interested in the Cuban market and its products.* Many additional
steps were taken, such as dialogue with the Cuban community.

However, once again U.S. perceptions of Cuban actions in several areas combined to block the possibility of restoring diplomatic relations.
The United States viewed negatively Cuba's policies in the UN (support
for Puerto Rico's independence and other policies to which the United
States was hostile), in the Non-Aligned Movement and its internationalist support for African and LAC nations. Artificial crises (the Shaba II
armed conflict in Zaire, Soviet delivery of Mig-23 aircraft to Cuba, and
the presence of a Soviet combat brigade) were reinforced by real ones,
such as the massive emigration of Cubans from the port of Mariel to the
United States in 1980 that constituted a hard blow to President Carter's
reelection prospects.

1979–1989: From Cuba's International Activism to the Fall of Soviet and East European Socialism

In the period 1979–1989, especially after Reagan's rise to the presidency (1981–1989), Cuba believed that the United States would carry
out a direct attack on the island. This perception came not only from the
statements of Reagan, his secretary of state Alexander Haig, and other
Reaganites but also from the rupture of the détente between the United
States and the Soviet Union.

All the contradictions between the United States and Cuba were
exacerbated. The revolution's leadership was confronted with the alternatives of either increasing its defensive capabilities or succumbing to
U.S. pressure for concessions. Cuba opted for the former. In addition, it
maintained its activism in the UN, in the Non-Aligned Movement—at
the New Delhi, Harare, and Belgrade summits—and continued carrying
out its internationalist policy in Africa and LAC. The change in Soviet
foreign policy that began in 1985 did not contribute to moderating the
Reagan administration's attitude toward Cuba but rather had the opposite effect.

In the neoconservative view during Reagan's Republican presidency,
at least until the beginning of perestroika in 1985, Cuba was perceived

---

* Among others, companies visiting Cuba or showing interest in its market were Coca-Cola,
General Motors, Ford, Caterpillar Inc., Abbott Laboratories, International Harvester, Boeing,
and Xerox.

as a Soviet spearhead, as a threat to U.S. security in the region, and as the source of subversion in Central America, the Caribbean, and Africa. Although during that time the United States, as already noted, maintained the Interests Sections and other previous agreements, and reached new accords with Cuba on the issue of migration, its regional policy, directly or indirectly, increased tensions with Cuba. Some relevant policy decisions and actions were the low-intensity war in Nicaragua, El Salvador, and other areas; the invasions of Grenada (1983) and Panama (1989); and the attacks on Cuba over human rights and democracy, among other issues.

In summary, since the late 1970s and early 1980s, the United States perceived that Cuba had prioritized its relations with national liberation movements and the Soviet Union over reestablishing Cuban-U.S. relations and that Carter's "concessions" had only served to strengthen and harden Cuba's positions in the international arena. This perception, along with other international factors, such as the disintegration of the Soviet Union and the socialist bloc, contributed to the growing hostility of the U.S. administrations of Reagan and his successor George H. W. Bush (1989–1993).

1989–2015: From the New Unipolar-Multipolar World Order to Reestablishing Diplomatic Relations

The **George H. W. Bush (1989–1993)** administration believed that Cuba would collapse at any moment. After the Panama invasion, the electoral defeat of the Sandinistas in Nicaragua, and the disintegration of the socialist bloc, the United States thought that the Cuban Revolution's days were numbered in a unipolar world where U.S. hegemony was undisputed after the Gulf War (1991). In a speech near the beginning of his term, Bush predicted that "I will be the first President of the United States to set foot on the soil of a free and democratic Cuba."[29]

Fidel expressed the Cuban government's perception of the Bush presidency in his speech at the IV Congress of the Cuban Communist Party (CCP) in 1991: Cuba was "a small island of Revolution in a virtually unipolar world, a few miles from hegemonic imperialism, and surrounded by capitalism on all sides."[30] But the strong support of the Cuban people for the revolution and its leadership ensured its survival; Cuba would not crumble as European socialism did and as Bush expected.

Between October 1993 and July 1994—prior to the "rafter" migration crisis in August 1994—the **Clinton administration (1993–2001)** tended to moderate the aggressive rhetoric of the Bush and Reagan administrations. Even after the crisis, immigration agreements were reached between the two countries. However, the shooting down of two civilian planes flown by Cuban counterrevolutionaries from the United States on February 24, 1996, produced a hardening of the Clinton policy toward Cuba. The main expression of this change was the adoption of the Helms-Burton Act in 1996.

In the aftermath of the downing of the planes, the Clinton administration now considered it necessary to change the political system in Cuba, something that the Cuban government was not willing to negotiate. The administration did not abandon its desire to "solve" the Cuban crisis through a peaceful "Nicaragua-style" transition in which the Cuban regime would be defeated in an election, but it did not rule out military intervention.

In Cuba's perception, there were no substantial differences in Cuba policy between the Republican governments of Reagan and Bush and the Democratic administration of Clinton, despite some increased flexibility by the latter toward the end of his term.

The administration of **George W. Bush (2001–2009)** viewed Cuba as a lesser threat, given the context created by the geopolitical complexities of its wars in Iraq and Afghanistan. Although he created the Commission for Assistance to a Free Cuba and adopted aggressive measures against Cuba, he showed some ambivalence. Unlike his Republican predecessors, in a speech on May 20, 2002, Bush expressed a willingness to work with the government of Fidel Castro.[31]

As the Cuban government perceived the situation, despite the militaristic and aggressive character of the Bush administration, the most dangerous moment for the revolution's survival had already passed. The results of economic reform were bearing fruit and the new relationship with Venezuela was helping the country overcome the difficult conditions experienced in the Special Period after the collapse of the Soviet Union and COMECON's disappearance. In addition, the threat of a direct military attack had faded due to a growing consensus among developed capitalist countries against a military attack on Cuba and in favor of a "soft transition." This, in addition to the significant amount of trade between Cuba and the United States, made military aggression seem less likely.

The Barack Obama Administration (2009–2015)

George W. Bush's foreign policy accelerated the decline of U.S. hegemony.[32] This decline continued during the Obama administration, given
the increasing divisions in the U.S. political system and the appearance
of actors such as the Tea Party. The divisions between Republicans and
Democrats were expressed not only in terms of the budget, bringing
the country to the edge of abyss, but also on international issues, with
negative consequences for U.S. hegemony. Obama proposed increasing China's participation in the International Monetary Fund (IMF)
from 3.8 to 6 percent, but this initiative was blocked by a small group
of Republican lawmakers, leading China to found its own institution,
the Asian Infrastructure Investment Bank (AIIB) in 2014. It invited the
UK, Australia, and several European Union countries to join, and they
became some of the fifty-four founders of the bank, despite U.S. disap-
proval. Recently, the Interamerican Development Bank (IDB) decided
to increase its financial ability to support the private sector in LAC and
proposed a capital increase of two billion dollars. All the shareholder
countries agreed, but the U.S. Congress and the bureaucrats of the
Treasury Department were opposed, thus diminishing U.S. influence in
this important institution. For this reason some analysts assert that the
main threat to U.S. hegemony does not come from Beijing but from its
own Congress.[33]

While in his first term Obama eschewed the aggressive rhetoric of the
Republican presidents and adopted measures that relaxed some aspects
of the blockade, he continued to condition dialogue with the island on
its conforming to the U.S. government's vision of human rights and
democracy, and he kept Cuba on the list of state sponsors of terrorism,
while demanding that it comply with the OAS Charter. As a result,
Cuba continued to perceive the U.S. government as an aggressive actor
that refused to recognize Cuba's sovereignty.

However, in his second term, Obama adopted the changed policy
that he announced on December 17, 2014, accepting the legitimacy of
the island's government and taking the steps that reestablished relations on July 20, 2015. Cuba viewed this as a radical change, for it
was the first time in eleven U.S. administrations that the legitimacy
of the Cuban Revolution and the failure of U.S. policy toward Cuba
were recognized.

NOTES

1. Alzugaray, "La actualización de la política exterior cubana."
2. Ibid.
3. Pérez, *Cuba in the American Imagination*, 32.
4. Monroe, "Annual Message."
5. Pérez, *Cuba in the American Imagination*, 32.
6. Ibid., 25.
7. Ibid., 26.
8. "Full Text of the Ostend Manifesto."
9. Pérez, *Cuba in the American Imagination*, 27.
10. Ibid., 28.
11. Ibid., 29.
12. Ibid., 34.
13. Ibid., 35.
14. "Full Text of the Ostend Manifesto."
15. Pérez, *Cuba in the American Imagination*, 39.
16. Ibid.
17. Ibid., 42–43.
18. Quoted in ibid., 43–44.
19. Ibid., 56.
20. Ibid., 58.
21. Wood, "Leonard Wood to Theodore Roosevelt."
22. Stone and Kuznik, *Untold History*, xxx.
23. Quoted in ibid., 40–41.
24. Martí, "Letter from José Martí to Manuel Mercado."
25. Buell and Foreign Policy Association, *Problems of the New Cuba*, 219.
26. F. Castro, "Histórica carta de Fidel a Celia."
27. Smith, *Closest of Enemies*, 62–63.
28. Franklin, *Cuban Foreign Relations*, 12.
29. G. H. W. Bush, "Remarks to Religious and Ethnic Groups."
30. F. Castro, "Discurso . . . en la Clausura del IV Congreso."
31. G. W. Bush, "Remarks Announcing the Initiative for a New Cuba."
32. López Segrera and Mojica, *¿Hacia dónde va?*
33. Naím, "Los autogoles de la superpotencia."

Chapter Three

From Close Enemies
to Distant Friends

This chapter's objectives are to review the main obstacles to reestablishing and normalizing relations between Cuba and the United States; to
identify the actors influencing the policies of both countries; to describe
the steps taken to restore diplomatic relations between December 17,
2014, and July 20, 2015; to explain the circumstances in both countries
that made restoring relations and moving toward normalization possible
as well as to identify the pending issues that still must be resolved; and
finally, to examine the main areas for cooperation between the two
countries on key issues of mutual interest.

MAIN OBSTACLES TO RESOLUTION
OF THE CUBAN-U.S. CONFLICT

On December 17, 2014, at the start of the process to reestablish diplomatic relations, Cuba and the United States were not only close enemies
but also exemplary neighbors in various areas, thanks to agreements
reached since the 1990s: direct professional and cooperative relations
between the military forces at the land border and between the Coast
Guards at sea; large-scale agricultural trade; agreements for effective
bilateral relations on migration issues; mutual appreciation of each
other's music, art, and culture; effective long-standing professional
relationships on hurricane tracking; and large diplomatic missions in
their respective capitals.[1]

What, then, had prevented the process of reestablishing relations from being started earlier? If the two countries were capable of reaching agreement on issues such as southern Africa and Central America, migration, the rafter crisis, the Elián González case, and other issues, why had they still not restored diplomatic relations? The only reason was that the United States would not accept Cuba's internal political regime.

The U.S. arguments for not reestablishing relations with the island varied over the years: between 1959 and 1990 Cuba was accused of being a threat to U.S. national security for being an ally of the Soviet Union and for exporting revolution to Africa and Latin America. After the disintegration of the Soviet Union and socialist bloc (1989–1991) and the negotiated settlement of the conflicts in southern Africa (1988) and Central America (1990), the United States brandished the argument that the island had to change its internal political system, something that had not been required of China and Vietnam.

Although Cuba had stopped being a "threat" to U.S. security after the fall of the Soviet Union, did not have military forces in Africa, and was not supporting insurgent forces in Latin America after the Central America peace accords were reached, the U.S. administrations continued their hard line because they were sure that Cuba would not survive without Soviet support. This conviction began to weaken during the Clinton administration and completely disappeared under Obama.

MAIN ACTORS INFLUENCING
U.S. POLICY TOWARD CUBA

While during the Cold War the key actor in U.S. policy toward Cuba was the governmental National Security Council, in the post–Cold War period most people consider that this role was assumed by the civilian exile organization the Cuban American National Foundation (CANF), which was believed to control the Florida vote and was capable of counteracting every initiative of the president and Congress to change policy toward Cuba. Curiously, this idea was mirrored in Cuba, for until December 17 many scholars of the issue stated that the "Cuban American mafia" controlled Washington's policy toward the island.[2] December 17 demonstrated that CANF, while influential in formulating U.S. policy toward Cuba, did not determine it. Those decisions were always made by the president, the Congress, and other U.S. power centers.

After December 17 and the resumption of relations on July 20, it became possible to empower an already existing anti-CANF lobby composed of Cuban American public figures and associations—some strongly anti-Castro—who oppose the blockade and supported restoring relations, foreseeing business opportunities on the island and smoother relations between Cubans on the island and those living in the United States.* Some suggest that even CANF could make a pragmatic turn after failing to prevent negotiations and the reestablishment of relations.†

A clear example of this trend among many anti-Castro Cuban Americans who approved Obama's policy is Republican businessman Carlos M. Gutiérrez, former president and chief executive officer of Kellogg, George W. Bush's ex-secretary of commerce (2005–2009), and currently copresident of the Albright Stonebridge Group; Gutiérrez wrote in a *New York Times* op-ed on June 23, 2015, "I believe that it is now time for Republicans and the wider American business community to stop fixating on the past and embrace a new approach to Cuba."[3]

STEPS TOWARD REESTABLISHING DIPLOMATIC RELATIONS (2014–2015)

The process of reestablishing diplomatic relations unfolded incrementally during the Obama administration.

Announcing the Start of Negotiations

On December 15, 2013, at the memorial service for Nelson Mandela, Barack Obama and Raúl Castro shook hands for the first time and spoke briefly. Their simultaneous December 17 announcement of the intent to

---

* In May 2015 the bipartisan lobby, Engage Cuba, was created, headed by James Williams, a political consultant who had once worked for John Kerry's presidential campaign. Behind this lobby lie powerful U.S. corporate interests such as Cargill, Procter and Gamble, and Caterpillar, among others. According to Engage Cuba's estimates, the Cuban market could eventually reach six billion dollars annually.

† There is strong opposition to the restoration of relations by CANF, three Cuban American senators, and four Cuban American members of the House of Representatives. However, according to more recent surveys, some 70 percent of Cuban Americans agree with reestablishing diplomatic relations. On Wednesday, February 11, 2015, the *Washington Post* published a letter to Congress signed by fifty public figures opposed to reestablishing and normalizing of relations with Cuba. Among the signatories were the mayor of Miami, an ex-chief of U.S. Interests Section in Cuba, and various Cuban dissident "leaders."

reestablish relations came almost exactly a year later. Because this mutual decision was the result of eighteen months of secret negotiations, the presidents' announcements came as a surprise.

The Vatican, through Pope Francis, supported and facilitated these negotiations by hosting a meeting between emissaries from both countries. This was the final step before a telephone conversation between the two presidents that preceded December 17. The presidents thanked both Pope Francis and the archbishop of Havana, Cardinal Jaime Ortega, for their key role in the negotiations.

Canada's prime minister, Stephen Harper, also facilitated the dialogue by hosting preliminary conversations in Canada and was likewise thanked for his support. Harper's involvement was important because his conservative government is similar to the U.S. Republican Party. However, it is noteworthy that, despite ups and downs, Canada has never broken relations with Cuba.

Reactions in the United States differed.* Republican leaders condemned the agreement, with some exceptions, such as Arizona senator Jeff Flake and Senator Rand Paul of Kentucky. The *Washington Post* published an editorial on December 17, 2014, stating, "Obama gives the Castro regime in Cuba an undeserved bailout" at a time when "the outlook for the Castro regime in Cuba was growing steadily darker."[4] However, the agreement had the support of U.S. society, Cuban Americans, the Catholic Church, the U.S. Chamber of Commerce, Human Rights Watch, and important agribusiness corporations.

Outside the United States, the reaction was very positive, both from Cubans and other Latin Americans. Ernesto Samper, secretary general of UNASUR; José Miguel Insulza, secretary general of the OAS; and President Juan Carlos Varela, host of the Seventh Summit of the Americas, held in April 2015 in Panama, expressed their support. The agreements also received strong support in Europe, Asia, and Africa.

Reaching this agreement—after more than half a century without relations—meant that both countries expected mutual benefit from it.

Obama's key argument for the agreement was that "these 50 years have shown that isolation has not worked," and "I do not believe we can keep doing the same thing for over five decades and expect a different result."[5]

---

* Hillary Clinton supported reestablishing relations with Cuba in a 2014 interview, prior to December 17. On December 18, 2014, she expressed her support of Obama's change in policy toward Cuba.

Obama's words do not mean that the United States has given up doing everything possible to change the Cuban political system—including efforts to erode and destroy the revolutionary process by other means—but that the method it has employed has collapsed. Thus, Obama does not question the unjust character of the blockade, only its ineffectiveness, and explains the new strategy, stating that "if we engage, we have the opportunity to influence the course of events at a time when there's going to be some generational change in that country."[6]

Since 2007, President Raúl Castro has repeatedly stated that he is willing to talk with the United States without preconditions but as a sovereign equal. Obama's December 17 change of policy, after fifty-four years of ineffective blockade, had the following objectives: prevent the Cuban government from using the blockade as an excuse for its economic problems; remove the justification for political measures appropriate for a country under siege; avoid U.S. isolation on votes on Cuba at the United Nations; and present a different image in Latin America.

President Raúl Castro declared,

President Obama's decision deserves the respect and acknowledgement of our people. . . . This in no way means that the heart of the matter has been solved. The economic, commercial, and financial blockade, which causes enormous human and economic damages to our country, must cease.

Though the blockade has been codified into law, the President of the United States has the executive authority to modify its implementation.

We propose to the Government of the United States the adoption of mutual steps to improve the bilateral atmosphere and advance toward normalization of relations between our two countries, based on the principles of International Law and the United Nations Charter.[7]

Just as Raúl's speech provided a more comprehensive synthesis than did Obama's, three days later, on December 20, before the National Assembly of People's Power, Raúl made it clear that "a very important step has been taken, but the essential problem still remains unresolved, which is the lifting of the economic, commercial and financial blockade against Cuba, that has been further tightened during the last few years, particularly in the area of financial transactions, through the application of skyrocketing and illegitimate fines on banks from several countries."[8] He continued by asserting that "we will demand respect for our system in the same way that we have never proposed that the United States change its political system."[9]

However, in his speech on December 17, Raúl had already expressed his willingness to discuss some of the thorniest issues between the two countries: "While acknowledging our profound differences, particularly on issues related to national sovereignty, democracy, human rights and foreign policy, I reaffirm our willingness to dialogue on all these issues."[10]

The first step following the agreement between the two countries was a prisoner exchange. Three of the Cuban Five, who were still in U.S. prisons, were freed and returned to the island where they are regarded as antiterrorist heroes. Alan Gross—a USAID contractor who was serving a sentence for subversive activities—as well as a Cuban spy recruited by the CIA and other prisoners the United States was interested in were freed, totaling fifty-three prisoners.

The U.S. president committed himself to reestablishing diplomatic relations, to reopening the embassy in Havana, to making it easier to travel and send remittances to Cuba, to developing relations between the two countries in very specific areas of mutual interest, and to evaluating the possibility of removing Cuba from the list of terrorist governments and organizations. Obama then instructed secretary of state John Kerry to begin the removal process that was finally concluded at the end of May 2015.* Obama also announced his willingness to take part in hemispheric meetings with Raúl Castro, saying in Spanish "Todos somos Americanos" (We are all Americans).[11]

Obama believes that the greater international opening for Cuba resulting from the restoration of relations will promote "democratic" change on the island. His policy consists of, on the one hand, continuing to pressure the government with the blockade and through the economic sanctions of the Helms-Burton Act, both still in effect. On the other hand, he attempts to project a positive image to ordinary Cubans and to the emerging private economy, authorizing an increase in the amount of remittances to make possible the financing of small, private businesses; export of telecommunications equipment and material to increase the number of Cubans who can access the Internet; and liberalization of the procedures for travel to Cuba to increase U.S. influence on the island. And Obama announced access to financial in-

---

* Cubans consider the U.S. Department of State's decision to include Cuba on the list of terrorist countries in 1982 to be unjust, and the reason—that it gave refuge to members of terrorist organizations from other countries—to be just a pretext.

struments (bank accounts, credit cards, etc.) that will allow the development of economic relations; negotiations about the maritime border among Cuba, the United States, and Mexico; and also, implicitly, a possible future agreement on civil aviation that would make increased flights possible.

Raúl Castro, for his part, made clear in his December 17 statement that despite being willing to "discuss and resolve our differences through negotiations," this would be done "without renouncing a single one of our principles." He continued:

> The heroic Cuban people, in the wake of serious dangers, aggressions, adversities, and sacrifices, have proven to be faithful and will continue to be faithful to our ideals of independence and social justice. Strongly united throughout these fifty-six years of revolution, we have kept our unswerving loyalty to those who died in defense of our principles since the beginning of our independence wars in 1868. Today, despite the difficulties, we have embarked on the task of updating our economic model in order to build a prosperous and sustainable socialism.[12]

The lesson is that the U.S. hard line has not broken Cuba and it is not likely that the new policy will bring about the collapse of its political system from within. China and Vietnam are relevant examples.

Undoubtedly, the agreement is a major victory for Cuba, one that buries the Cold War logic that prevailed until December 17. Just as the United States initially isolated Cuba, now the situation has been reversed. After more than fifty-four years, it is the United States that is isolated, especially in Latin America and the Caribbean.

Cubans view this as Obama's most positive foreign policy decision, in an area where so many unsound decisions have been made. If the Republicans in Congress are too intransigent, this can only push Obama to go further. In an interview with the Associated Press, after the agreement, he stated that he did not rule out a similar move with Iran, even though it would be more difficult.[13]

According to William LeoGrande, the new relationship between Cuba and the United States represents "a decisive break with the past. Since 1959 (with only brief attempts at normalizing relations in the 1970s), U.S. policy has been aimed at forcing regime change in Cuba through economic, and, at times, even military, coercion. President Obama has abandoned that policy and replaced it with one of engagement and normality."[14]

On January 26, 2015, more than a month after Obama and Raúl Castro's announcement, Fidel Castro referred to the negotiation process for the first time in a letter to the Federation of University Students: "I do not trust the policy of the United States, nor have I exchanged one word with them, though this does not in any way signify a rejection of a peaceful solution to conflicts or threats of war."[15] Later he pointed out, "The President of Cuba has taken pertinent steps in accordance with the prerogatives and powers that are granted to him by the National Assembly and the Communist Party of Cuba."[16]

Some analysts think that, while Fidel agreed with the negotiation process in principle, perhaps he disapproved of specific aspects or steps that were taken. It is widely believed that after Fidel's comments, Cuba's position hardened.

The Negotiation Process and Reestablishing Relations

Between December 17, 2014, and May 21, 2015, four rounds of negotiations on reestablishing relations were held, two in Havana and two in Washington.

The *first round* took place in Havana on January 21 and 22, 2015. The assistant secretary of state for western hemispheric affairs, Roberta Jacobson, led the U.S. delegation. On the Cuban side, Josefina Vidal Ferreiro, director general for U.S. relations in the Ministry of Foreign Relations, oversaw the talks. On the first day, they returned to migration issues—including Cuban rejection of the Cuban Adjustment Act for encouraging emigration—and on the second, discussed the process of restoring relations and reopening embassies.

After concluding this first round, in a press conference at the Havana residence of the chief of the U.S. Interests Section, Roberta Jacobson acknowledged that despite the new measures announced on December 17, "Our ends remain the same."[17] In other words, tactics were revised in pursuit of the same strategic objective—to bring about a change in the Cuban model, so it would more closely resemble the United States. She noted "areas of deep disagreement" with the Cuban government but recognized that these need not constitute an obstacle to restoring diplomatic relations and reopening their respective embassies.[18]

In a January 23 interview with the Associated Press, Josefina Vidal stated that Cuba was prepared to eliminate restrictions on the movement of U.S. diplomats on the island, as the United States had demanded, if and when its representatives stopped "organizing, training, supporting, encouraging, financing and supplying small groups of people that act against the Cuban government and really represent the interests of the United States inside our country. That is action that is not acceptable."[19] Although she declined to express it as a "condition," she noted that allowing diplomats greater freedom of movement "is associated with better behavior."[20]

On February 27, the same chief negotiators led the *second round* of talks in Washington. The Cuban representatives reiterated the importance of resolving several issues in order to create an appropriate context for reestablishing relations and opening embassies. They emphasized removing Cuba from the list of "state sponsors of international terrorism" and providing financial services to the Cuban Interests Section in Washington, which had lacked access to a bank for more than a year due to the blockade and Cuba's inclusion on the terrorism sponsor list.

Likewise, the Cuban delegation insisted on the need to ensure compliance with the principles of international law and the Vienna Convention on Diplomatic and Consular Relations as the basis of future diplomatic relations and the operation of the respective embassies. Specifically, they emphasized meeting the norms regarding the functioning of diplomatic missions and the behavior of their personnel—respect for national laws and nonintervention in the internal affairs of states.

Furthermore, they clarified details about the bilateral technical visits and meetings that would be held in the following weeks about issues such as civil aviation, human trafficking, telecommunications, migration fraud prevention, and regulatory changes to modify implementation of the blockade.

In press conferences after the meetings, Vidal and Jacobson emphasized the professional, respectful, and constructive climate in which the talks unfolded.

The *third round of negotiations* took place in the strictest secrecy on March 16 in Havana, again led by Vidal and Jacobson. Although the United States wanted to reestablish diplomatic relations before the Summit of the Americas in Panama on April 10 and 11, Cuba apparently would not agree until it was removed from the list of terrorist countries and Cuba's Interests Section in Washington was given access to a bank to carry out its financial operations.

Between the third and fourth round, on April 8, before leaving for Jamaica and then the Summit of the Americas in Panama, Obama and Raúl Castro held their second telephone conversation. Then, on April 10, they greeted each other during the summit's inaugural ceremony, and the following day they met for an hour and twenty minutes to discuss reestablishing relations. Previously, U.S. secretary of state John Kerry had met in Panama for three hours with his Cuban counterpart, and both declared that the discussion had been respectful and constructive.

A month earlier, on March 8, President Obama had issued an executive order that identified Venezuela as a threat and imposed sanctions on several Venezuelan officials (discussed more fully in a later section). The measure was widely denounced in Latin America. The concern that this executive order would create conflicts at the summit was unfounded. Before his arrival at the Summit, Obama—although not withdrawing the executive order—modified his initial statement saying, "We do not believe that Venezuela poses a threat to the United States, nor is the US a threat to the Venezuelan government."[21] Raúl expressed his total solidarity with Venezuela, but neither his position nor Obama's created a conflict capable of derailing the U.S.-Cuban negotiations about restoring relations.

On April 14, Josefina Vidal announced that President Obama had submitted to Congress the certification required for rescission of Cuba's designation as a state sponsor of terrorism, which would take effect in forty-five days. The Cuban government considered this a just decision; it maintained that the country should never have been included on the list since it is Cuba that has been a victim of hundreds of terrorist acts, which have cost the lives of 3,478 people and disabled 2,099 Cuban citizens.

On May 21 and 22, Cuba and the United States held their *fourth round* of diplomatic negotiations in Washington. The Cuban Ministry of Foreign Relations specified that this round of talks would focus on "the operation of diplomatic missions and the behavior of their officials."[22] When the talks concluded, despite both sides recognizing "progress," they had not set a date for reestablishing relations and reopening embassies.

Two key pending issues had already been resolved: after more than a year of unsuccessful searching, the Cuban Interests Section in Washington had found a bank to handle its transactions in U.S. territory—Stonegate, a small bank in Florida. Furthermore, on May 29, one week after the fourth round was completed, Cuba was removed from the list of terrorist countries. Apparently the only thorny issue left pending was the movement of diplomats in both countries and their activities in that capacity.

Then on July 1, 2015, Cuba and the United States announced that on July 20, their respective Interests Sections would be elevated to the rank of embassies, ending almost half a century of diplomatic rupture between the two countries. That same day, in a statement to the press, President Obama noted that "there are Americans who want to travel to Cuba and American businesses who want to invest in Cuba" and stated, "I've called on Congress to take steps to lift the embargo that prevents Americans from travelling or doing business in Cuba."[23]

Also on July 1, the interim Cuban minister of foreign relations, Marcelino Medina González, received the chief of the U.S. Interests Section in Havana, Jeffrey DeLaurentis, who gave him a letter from President Obama, dated June 30, addressed to armed forces general Raúl Castro, president of the Councils of States and Ministers, in which he confirmed the decision to restore diplomatic relations between the two countries and open permanent diplomatic missions in their respective capitals on July 20, 2015.

That same day in Washington, the chief of the Cuban Interests Section, José Ramón Cabañas Rodríguez, was received in the Department of State by the deputy secretary of state, Anthony Blinken, to whom he gave a letter from Raúl to Obama, dated July 1, in which he confirmed the Republic of Cuba's decision to reestablish diplomatic relations with the United States.

In his letter, President Obama affirmed,

I am pleased to confirm, following high-level discussions between our two governments, and in accordance with international law and practice, that the United States of America and the Republic of Cuba have decided to re-establish diplomatic relations and permanent diplomatic missions in our respective countries on July 20, 2015. This is an important step forward in the process of normalizing relations between our two countries and peoples that we initiated last December.[24]

Similarly, the first paragraph of President Raúl Castro's letter stated,

Consistent with the announcements made on December 17, 2014, and the high level discussions between our two governments, I am pleased to address this letter to you in order to confirm that the Republic of Cuba has agreed to re-establish diplomatic relations with the United States of America and open permanent diplomatic missions in our respective countries on July 20, 2015.[25]

On July 1, the official Communist Party newspaper *Granma* published a "Statement by the Revolutionary Government" referring to the exchange of letters between Raúl and Obama "through which they confirmed the decision to re-establish diplomatic relations between the two countries and open permanent diplomatic missions in their respective capitals, from July 20, 2015."[26]

The statement continues,

> That same day, the official opening ceremony of the Embassy of Cuba in Washington will be held, in the presence of a Cuban delegation led by Foreign Minister Bruno Rodríguez Parrilla and composed of distinguished representatives of Cuban society. . . . With the re-establishment of diplomatic relations and the opening of embassies, the first phase concludes of what will be a long and complex process towards the normalization of bilateral ties. . . . There can be no normal relations between Cuba and the United States as long as the economic, commercial and financial blockade . . . is maintained. . . . To achieve normalization it will also be indispensable that the territory illegally occupied by the Guantanamo Naval Base is returned, that radio and television transmissions to Cuba that are in violation of international norms and harmful to our sovereignty cease, that programs aimed at promoting subversion and internal destabilization are eliminated, and that the Cuban people are compensated for the human and economic damages caused by the policies of the United States.[27]

On July 20, 2015, both countries' embassies, in Washington and Havana, were opened, beginning a new era between the two nations, in which they will move from being close enemies to neighbors that, although distant at the start, can create mutually beneficial relations.

CIRCUMSTANCES IN THE UNITED STATES THAT FACILITATED THE PROCESS

Factors Favoring Negotiation and Reestablishing Relations

The way the U.S. and Cuban leadership and political classes understood historical developments in the new international era offered unprecedented opportunities for negotiation.

The disintegration of the socialist bloc and the Soviet Union (1991) and Raúl Castro's assumption of leadership (2006) have not prevented maintaining social peace and minimal economic performance in Cuba, nor seriously fractured the consensus.

This meant that the U.S. sectors that had rejected taking the same approach to negotiating with Cuba that had been used with China became willing to resume diplomatic relations and even to reach full normalization. The real political will now demonstrated by President Obama and broad sectors of U.S. political class and society had never before existed in regard to Cuba.

Negotiations between the two countries in the 1970s, 1980s, 1990s, and into the twenty-first century were characterized by a refusal to go beyond resolving specific issues of primary importance to the United States—that is, plane hijackings, migration, the conflict in South-West Africa, the Central American conflict, and the Elián González case. To transcend this negative stance, the United States would have to give up its goal of substantially changing the island's internal political regime and agree to address the political, economic, military, legal, technical, and other bilateral issues whose resolution would permit true normalization. Clearly December 17 and July 20 meant that the United States now had the political will to recognize Cuban sovereignty and no longer demand that it change its domestic economic, political, and social systems in exchange for full normalization.

The factors, among others, that led the U.S. government to abandon the negative attitudes noted above and go forward with negotiations and reestablishing relations are as follows:

1. Cuba has not fallen despite the collapse of European socialism. An invasion is not advisable because of the multiple kinds of losses that it would cause the United States. Is it not better to restore diplomatic relations and advance toward normalization by lifting the blockade?
2. The United States could put into effect an alternative policy of attempting to undermine Cuban socialism from within. Especially now that Cuba is rapidly reinserting itself into international market relations, this policy would no longer deprive U.S. transnational corporations of the billion dollars annually they would gain from the island but that currently flow to corporations from other countries.
3. Cuba is no longer a "threat," as a "pawn" of the Soviet Union, nor is it present in the "Cold War" theaters of operation in Central America and Africa.

4. In the multilateral arena, only the United States, Israel, and some small, less influential countries vote against the annual UN resolution denouncing the blockade. Otherwise, the entire international community opposes it.

5. Fidel Castro and then Raúl Castro have achieved political stability and consensus (even in the most difficult situations), something that a "Cuban" president from the Cuban American National Foundation—incapable of uniting the Cuban community in the United States—could not do in a Cuba where capitalism had been restored after a costly invasion.

6. For the United States, a politically stable Cuba with a not insignificant market is preferable to a country experiencing civil war and endemic conflicts.

7. After the reestablishment and normalization of relations, Cuba could become an even greater stabilizing factor in the region, due to the importance that a new relationship of equality with the United States would have for the island.

8. Cuba has played a major role as host for negotiations between the government of Colombia and the FARC (Revolutionary Armed Forces of Colombia—People's Army). Could it not also help mediate tensions between the United States and other countries in the region, especially Venezuela?

9. To restore diplomatic relations with Cuba, the island need not have a democracy identical to that of the developed Western countries. Why demand of Cuba what has not been asked of China or Vietnam? Why this double standard?

10. The high level of education of the Cuban population, the low crime rate, and the quality of its public health care are other factors that make the island attractive for U.S. investors.

To summarize, Cuba's gradual economic recovery has been a key factor leading to the U.S. shift in policy, along with other factors, such as fear of a migration crisis; practically unanimous condemnation of the blockade by the international community through UN resolutions; the persistent rejection by Latin America, the European Union—Cuba's main trade partners since 1994—and Canada of this anti-Cuba policy; the need to reconfigure U.S. international relations in response to Russia and China's growing presence in Latin America; the search for a new U.S. image at the Summit of the Americas that would allow it to modernize its forms of domination in the region; and the ever-increasing rejection by diverse sectors in the United States of this policy that affects the U.S. people and majority sectors of its business community, who do not want to be excluded from a guaranteed, nearby market with innumerable other advantages.

In regard to democracy, the different perceptions of their political systems do not imply hostility between the U.S. and Cuban peoples, because according to recent polls the majority of U.S. public opinion has changed to favor restoring diplomatic relations and lifting the blockade. Although Cubans find U.S. policy toward Cuba highly objectionable, they also admire and value many aspects of U.S. culture and technology. Many consider that along with the influence of African and Spanish culture, U.S. culture, through films, music, and technology, has been very influential and greatly appreciated on the island, which contributes to bringing the two peoples closer together.

Once diplomatic relations were reestablished on July 20, two essential steps to fully normalize them are lifting the blockade and returning the Guantánamo base to Cuba.

To review: What led to a change in the U.S. negotiating strategy, which until December 17 was limited to considering specific, limited issues, without addressing the reestablishment of diplomatic relations? We have already referred to a set of circumstances and factors that created a very favorable conjuncture for the United States to change its policy toward Cuba, at least at the tactical level. Polls have shown that the restoration of relations, normalization, and the end of the blockade are supported by the overwhelming majority of U.S. public opinion, including Cuban Americans, by all the governments of Latin America and the Caribbean, and by U.S. allies such as Canada and the European Union. All these actors recognize that a reform process is being carried out under the presidency of Raúl Castro, without this rupturing the consensus or creating political instability on the island.

Another factor is that reestablishing relations with Cuba represents an undeniable foreign policy success for Obama in a context where he can claim few others. The new scenario in Latin America following the formation of CELAC (Community of Latin American and Caribbean States) is also especially important because the United

States can no longer consider or treat the region as its backyard. Restoring relations with Cuba is a key step for projecting a different image in the region.

The Cuban political class and its leadership are prepared to accept the logic of economic interdependence as a path to definitively overcome dependence in this sphere, especially in a world where they recognize that socialism is neither irreversible nor rapidly advancing and where the alternative is to increasingly insert itself into the international and regional economy or remain at the margins of history. This new Cuban understanding prioritizes more than ever reaching a definitive solution to the conflict with the United States but without renouncing the essence of the nation.

Recent Polls

In April 2009, a CNN opinion poll revealed that 64 percent of U.S. respondents thought that the U.S. government should lift its prohibition on U.S. citizens traveling to Cuba, and 71 percent agreed that the United States should reestablish diplomatic relations with the island.

A *Washington Post–ABC News* poll on December 23, 2014, showed that 64 percent favored restoring diplomatic relations with Cuba. By political party, 77 percent of Democrats supported this change in policy compared to 49 percent of Republicans. Among Hispanics, 75 percent approved restoring diplomatic relations with Cuba, and 29 percent were opposed. Support for lifting the economic and trade embargo with Cuba rose to 68 percent, up eleven points from 2009. Moreover, 74 percent want to end restrictions on U.S. citizens traveling to the island, a nineteen-point increase from 2009.

According to a Pew Research Center poll, carried out January 7–11, 2014, 63 percent approved Obama's decision to restore relations with Cuba that just 28 percent opposed. Furthermore, 66 percent supported lifting the embargo, and only 28 percent disagreed. Thirty-two percent considered that Cuba would become more democratic in the coming years, while 60 percent believed that it would stay the same.

An Associated Press–GfK survey on February 4, 2015, showed 45 percent in favor of restoring diplomatic relations between the two countries with only 15 percent against. Sixty percent said Washington should end its trade embargo on Cuba, and only 35 percent believed it should be maintained. Furthermore, 12 percent of U.S. residents stated that they would be likely or very likely to visit the island if they could obtain a tourist visa, while another 17 percent indicated a moderate likelihood of traveling there in that case. Almost a third of those who approved the opening of relations with Havana said that they would probably visit the Caribbean island if they could.

A Gallup poll of February 20, 2015, revealed that the U.S. public has a more positive view of Cuba today than at any time during the last two decades. Forty-six percent reported having a favorable opinion, eight percentage points higher than the year before and well above the 10 percent favorable opinion in 1996. Polls over more than forty years show that U.S. public opinion has always tended to support restoring diplomatic relations with Havana, except immediately after the approval of the Helms-Burton Act in 1996, when support fell to 40 percent. It soon rebounded significantly, reaching 70 percent in 1999. Since then, restoring relations has continued to enjoy majority support.

In terms of U.S. public opinion about the blockade, 59 percent favor lifting it. This is the highest percentage found by Gallup since it first included a specific question on this topic in 1999. Likewise, 59 percent support totally ending restrictions on travel to Cuba by U.S. citizens.

A March 11, 2015, survey by the Beyond the Beltway project, an initiative of the consultants Benenson Strategy Group and SKD Knickerbocker, showed 64 percent of all voters supported ending the blockade, including 74 percent of Democrats, 51 percent of Republicans, and 64 percent of independents.

By an even wider margin, 72 percent of voters favored having diplomatic relations with Cuba, more trade, and more travel to the island. Of those, 64 percent of Republicans younger than fifty recognized that the recent political changes serve the interests of both the U.S. and Cuban peoples.

Furthermore, a March 2015 poll carried out in Cuba by the private firm Bendixen & Amandi, using a countrywide sample of 1,200 residents, showed that 97 percent of respondents believed that normalization of relations is good for Cuba, 96 percent wanted the embargo lifted, 89 percent believed that Obama should visit Cuba, and 83 percent thought that Raúl should visit the United States.[28] Overall, as these five polls demonstrate, Obama's policy is consistent with what the majority of U.S. voters want.

CIRCUMSTANCES IN CUBA THAT
FACILITATED THE PROCESS

For the United States, deciding to reestablish and normalize relations would have been more difficult with Fidel Castro as president than with Raúl, because of the much greater emotional baggage associated with negotiating with Fidel. Another important condition for the United States was that Cuba demonstrate its clear political will to prioritize the negotiations and not sabotage progress, as occurred, in the U.S. view, with Cuba's military presence in Angola (1975) and Ethiopia (1977), opening the port of Mariel for emigration (1980), or the downing of the planes (1996). These two conditions were fully met starting in 2006 when Raúl replaced Fidel as president.

While the policy changes introduced by Raúl Castro have not advanced quickly enough in the U.S. view, it is also clear that since he assumed office, rather than more of the same, important changes are underway in both the political (freedom to migrate, greater freedom of expression for alternative views, etc.) and the economic (rapid development of private businesses) spheres. In addition, Cuba needs new economic alternatives that reduce the amount of its trade with Venezuela, which has been seriously affected by the drop in oil prices.*

The government's "updating of the economic model" requires a comprehensive development strategy, which includes a higher rate of foreign investment, intended to eliminate dependence on exporting professional services and on remittances, as we have previously analyzed in another book. Cuban professionals' low salaries lead to an emigration that deprives the country of its most valuable social and human capital.†
Finding a solution to the dual currency issue is urgent in order to curb the high rate of emigration of skilled workers and professionals.‡

---

* Cuba receives one hundred thousand barrels of oil daily from Venezuela—a quantity that was reduced by almost 50 percent in September 2014—in exchange for more than thirty thousand doctors, health-care personnel, and specialists in various areas such as education and sports. Cooperation began in 2000 with 17 projects that by 2010 grew to 285 projects and contracts for three billion dollars.

† The Cuban population on the island is 11,242,621. In 2013 there were 2,013,155 Cuban immigrants to the United States. It is estimated that Cuban immigrants total some 2,500,000.

‡ The dual currency system was introduced during the Special Period and involved the circulation of Cuban Pesos (CUPs) and Convertible Cuban Pesos (CUCs). The CUC was pegged to the U.S. dollar and was worth more than twenty times the CUP. Most Cubans, including professionals such as doctors, were paid in CUPs. This gave economic advantages to those Cubans who had access to CUCs, especially those working in the tourist sector. See "Desafíos económicos de Cuba"; López Segrera, *La Revolución Cubana*.

Another important factor is the generational change underway in Cuba and the urgency felt by Raúl Castro and the historic leadership to leave a viable economy and country for new generations. After his reelection in 2013, Raúl announced that he will leave the presidency at the end of his second term in 2018.

In addition, the aging of Cuban exiles, with the older generations more reluctant to restore relations than the younger ones, has favored policy change but has not been the determining factor. The majority of the new generations of Cuban Americans support the restoration of relations and the end of the blockade.

FROM REESTABLISHING RELATIONS TO FULL NORMALIZATION

As already emphasized, December 17 involved a number of essential changes in U.S. policy toward Cuba:

1. For the first time, the United States acknowledged the failure of the policy followed by eleven U.S. administrations and accepted the legitimacy of the Cuban government. As Obama stated on December 17, "We will end an outdated approach that, for decades, has failed to advance our interests, and instead we will begin to normalize relations between our two countries."[29]
2. The United States authorized expanded travel and increases in remittances and bilateral trade. This meant that the Treasury Department would facilitate banking operations and allow the use of U.S. debit and credit cards in Cuba. One effect of the changes will be the increased ability of Americans to provide training and other support to the emerging Cuban private sector, which includes about five hundred thousand workers. Moreover, the Commerce Department will relax current export limits on a variety of products that will aid the growth of small Cuban businesses, such as construction firms, agricultural companies, car repair shops, and others.
3. The new policy will allow the sale of technology to modernize the Internet.
4. Obama requested the State Department to review the designation of Cuba as a state sponsor of terrorism, and on May 29, 2015, Cuba was removed from the list.
5. Rounds of talks to reestablish diplomatic relations were begun.

The significance of December 17 is that hostility was replaced with constructive dialogue between two sovereign states on an equal footing. Three essential measures were adopted after December 17: jointly announcing the start of a process to restore diplomatic relations; developing rounds of talks; and removing Cuba from the list of terrorist countries. The next key step was to reestablish diplomatic relations with the opening of embassies in Washington and Havana on July 20, 2015. Even before the opening of the embassies, progress was being made in areas of mutual interest.

However, while reestablishing relations represents a great step forward that gives a key role to diplomacy as opposed to coercion, which had been dominant up to that point, this does not mean that the instruments of aggression against Cuba are automatically dismantled. Going from mere restoration of diplomatic relations to true normalization will require moving forward on a long and complex trajectory.

The elimination of the trade and financial blockade—which Obama has identified as something to resolve with Congress once there has been progress on other issues—is key to this process and would mean a significant advance, but until then there could be progress through a multitude of agreements on the economy, security, migration, public health, and education.

Relations between Cuba and the United States have never been normal, since prior to 1959 the island was a neocolony of the United States, whose ambassador had more power than the Cuban president. The United States has treated the issue of Cuba more as a domestic matter than as an international relation with a sovereign country. Therefore, the United States would have to stop considering Cuba as a country with limited sovereignty and accept the same relationship with it as with Brazil, Canada, or France. The asymmetry that exists between the two countries would no longer be transferred to the political arena. Normalization would require clear and explicit U.S. willingness to eliminate the blockade, the Cuban Adjustment Act, the subversive USAID, and other activities detrimental to Cuban sovereignty. Just as LeoGrande has made a list of things that Cuba should do (see below), the United States should also show through concrete actions that all the problems of mutual interest could be resolved through diplomatic dialogue and without coercion.

To review, there are certain Cuban demands that the United States should have met during the negotiations to reestablish relations—

especially removing the country from the list of terrorist countries—and others that it should comply with now following July 20, in order to fully normalize them: unconditionally eliminating all economic sanctions and the blockade; allowing foreign banks to do business with Cuba without U.S. sanctions; returning the Guantánamo base; providing compensation for the damages caused by the blockade; ending transmissions of Radio and TV Martí; and repealing the Cuban Adjustment Act that, since 1966, treats Cuban migrants that set foot on U.S. territory as refugees.

Moreover, as already noted, of the many foreign policy conflicts that Obama must confront—the Middle East, Russia, and others—the one with Cuba offers the best conditions for obtaining rapid results and demonstrating an unquestioned success domestically while simultaneously changing the U.S. image in Latin America and the Caribbean.

The conflict between the United States and Venezuela seems to have adversely affected the process of negotiating the reestablishment of Cuban-U.S. relations, but it did not derail it, as was seen during the Summit of the Americas. On March 9, 2015, Obama issued an executive order that proclaimed a "national emergency" due to "an unusual and extraordinary threat to the national security and foreign policy of the United States" and stated that, as a result, seven high-level Venezuelan officials would be prohibited from entering the United States.[30] Obama's reaction, situated in the framework of an aggressive policy toward Venezuela, was a response to President Nicolás Maduro's decision in February to cut U.S. diplomatic personnel in Venezuela by 80 percent and ban seven congressmen and leaders from entering the country, claiming they were involved in plotting a coup. Cuban ambassador Bruno Rodríguez visited Maduro on March 14 and declared that the United States could not have a policy of "the carrot" for Cuba and "the stick" for Venezuela.[31] Furthermore, on March 17, 2015, Raúl supported Venezuela in the ALBA Summit in Caracas, where he stated,

U.S. imperialism has attempted, without success, practically all possible formulas to destabilize and subvert the Bolivarian Chavista revolution. . . . The arbitrary, aggressive, unjustified executive order issued by the President of the United States regarding the Bolivarian Republic of Venezuela's government, describing it as a threat to its national security, shows that the United States is able to sacrifice the peace and the direction of hemispheric and regional relations, for reasons of domination and

domestic politics. . . . The United States must understand once and for all
that it is impossible to seduce or buy Cuba, or intimidate Venezuela. Our
unity is indestructible. . . . We will reject with determination any attempt
to isolate or threaten Venezuela.[32]

On March 5, 2015, political scientist William LeoGrande proposed
"five things that Cuba can do to move the normalization process forward without compromising its sovereignty."[33]

1. "Send a broadly representative civil society delegation to the Summit of the Americas." Cuba did this on its own initiative with great
   success.
2. "Cooperate with the International Committee of the Red Cross
   and the United Nations Human Rights Council." This will make it
   "harder . . . for opponents of normalization to wield the human rights
   issue to derail the process."
3. "Expand internet access" through agreements with U.S. telecommunications companies.
4. "Facilitate U.S. trade with the private sector." The state should pre-
   pare to meet the challenges that large-scale U.S. trade with Cuba's
   growing private sector will present.
5. "Work with the United States to refocus democracy programs." This
   involves "an opportunity to reorient the programs away from regime
   change, instead focusing them on supporting authentic ties between
   Cuban and U.S. civil society."

While LeoGrande's proposals for Cuban actions to advance from reestablishing relations to normalization are interesting, they should also
deal with what the United States could do, in all areas, to help speed up
full normalization after July 20.

At that point, President Obama had only two years left in his presidency and Raúl Castro only three. The two presidents' pace for moving
forward will shape the future of relations between the two countries
once their successors take power.

MAIN AREAS FOR COOPERATION

Reestablishing and eventually fully normalizing Cuban-U.S. relations
offer the possibility for mutually beneficial cooperation in many areas.

Economy

Four watershed events that condition economic relations between the two countries were the United States establishing the blockade in 1961, the fall of the socialist bloc and the Soviet Union in 1991, and the events of December 17 and July 20, at a time when Cuba is making efforts to "update the economic model." The structural reforms being carried out in Cuba need to be responsive to the new dynamic created by December 17 and July 20. After the Department of the Treasury and the Department of Commerce's Bureau of Industry and Security published revised rules regulating exports and travel to Cuba on January 15, 2015, proposals and applications to invest in the island have increased. A report issued in late April 2015 estimates that investment applications grew 757 percent since December 17 and that three hundred foreign companies have expressed interest.[34]

Cuba has trade relations with some seventy countries and also received major investments from Canada (nickel, oil, and tourism), Spain (tourism), China (various fields), and Venezuela (oil refinery and hundreds of projects). Despite this, the blockade has had serious adverse effects: foreign banks have suffered severe U.S. sanctions for doing business with the island, and there are surcharges on U.S. merchandise purchased through third countries as well as higher shipping costs.

Since 2001, Cuban-U.S. economic relations have consisted of the sale of food and medicine to Cuba, following approval of the Trade Sanction Reform and Export Expansion Act in 2000 during the Clinton administration. In 2006, 96 percent of rice and 70 percent of poultry came from the United States. In 2008, the United States became Cuba's main supplier of food and its fourth-largest trading partner. However, this commerce was subject to a series of restrictions: purchases by Cuba required authorization from the Treasury Department; transactions could not be made in U.S. dollars and had to be paid in advance and in cash; and merchandise had to be transported on ships contracted by the vendors in the United States.

Between 2001 and 2013 Cuba purchased poultry, corn, soy, wheat, and animal feed from U.S. agribusiness, reaching a maximum of 598 million dollars in 2008, for a total of 4.98 billion dollars through 2013.

This flexibility in agricultural trade did not eliminate the punitive effects of the blockade. In 2014, the French bank PNB Paribas had to pay a nine-billion-dollar fine for violating the embargo on Cuba, Iran, and Sudan. Also in 2014, the United States fined the German Commerzbank

1.7 billion dollars for violation of sanctions on transactions with Cuba, Iran, or Sudan.

According to estimates in 2005, free trade with Cuba would have significant advantages for the U.S. economy. Depending on Cuba's GDP, Cuban exports to the United States could reach 4.21 billion dollars annually, and imports from the United States amount to 9.47 billion dollars by 2013. This relationship with Cuba would mean the creation of between 315,621 and 845,621 U.S. jobs over twenty years. Ten years later in 2015, the amount of trade and related jobs would be much greater.[35]

While reestablishing relations and lifting the blockade will facilitate more favorable economic relations for Cuba with the rest of the world and particularly with the United States, Cuba's foreign trade should not become highly concentrated with the latter, as advantageous as improved Cuban-U.S. relations may be.

Moreover, the Cuban government seeks free trade with the United States without any restrictions. However, the recent regulations promulgated after December 17 tend to limit trade relations to the nonstate sector.

The immediate economic impact of December 17 will be felt most in two areas: significant increases in remittances and in travel to Cuba by U.S. residents. It is foreseeable that remittances could increase from 1.5 billion dollars annually to no less than 2 billion since the officially authorized level of remittances increased from two thousand annually per person to eight thousand U.S. dollars.* Despite the restrictions on travel to Cuba prior to December 17, more than 163,106 Cuban Americans traveled to Cuba in 2006, increasing to 386,367 in 2014, 2.4 times as many. Furthermore, under the other eleven categories of authorized travel, 36,808 U.S. citizens traveled to Cuba in 2006, a number that increased by 2.5 times to 91,400 in 2014.[36] With the expected increase, the estimated number of tourists would fluctuate between five hundred thousand and one million, which would mean an additional gross income of between 750 thousand and 1.4 billion dollars annually.†

It is likely that different forms of tourism, such as for health care, nature, fishing, and cruise ships, will experience a boom, and one of the

---

* It is estimated that about 25 percent of the Cuban population receives remittances, and about 50 percent of their value is considered working capital for the private and cooperative sector.

† In 2014, before December 17, three bills were presented in the U.S. Senate to increase travel by U.S. residents and exports to Cuba.

challenges Cuba will face will be to increase hotel capacity. The emerging private sector will be a good partner in this boom.

It is clear, therefore, that the major areas of interest for U.S. businesspeople, at least in the short term, will be tourism, hospitality and travel services, maritime transport, telecommunications, construction materials, and agriculture. Construction materials will be the most in demand because of the island's great housing deficit. There will also be high demand in the urban transport and railroad sectors.

Other particularly noteworthy areas of potential cooperation are oil production and exploration (the island annually produces around 3.5 million tons of oil); the nickel industry (Cuba has the fifth-largest reserves in the world); agriculture; banking; infrastructure and housing construction; and foreign direct investment. Cuba needs investment of between 1.8 and 2.3 billion euros annually, and to meet this objective, a new law on foreign investment was approved in April 2014, effective June 28, and allowed investment in all sectors except health, education, and the armed forces. It also provided for Cuba's entry into international (International Monetary Fund [IMF] and World Bank) and regional financial organizations (Interamerican Development Bank).

In the telecommunications sector, in February 2015 an initial agreement was signed between the Cuban state telecommunications company ETECSA and the U.S. company IDT that would allow direct communication between the two countries.

On each trip, visitors returning from Cuba can import Cuban products valued up to four hundred dollars, one hundred of which can be alcohol and tobacco. In addition, Cuba could export to the United States 270 million dollars in tobacco products per year, equivalent to 30 percent of the premium tobacco it produces. There are also excellent prospects for the sale of Cuban rum. Other promising fields include pharmaceutical products from the biotechnology sector, the software industry, and health-care services.

After December 17, other measures to facilitate economic exchanges include the use of credit cards for visitors from the United States and banking services for merchants. Cuba will also benefit in other, less quantifiable, ways, such as liberalizing some exports from the United States (despite the blockade not having been eliminated), commercial imports of certain goods and services produced in Cuba by independent entrepreneurs, and commercial sale of specific kinds of communication software, hardware, and services.

Given the enormous investment in education made by the revolutionary government, Cuba has a large, highly skilled labor force, including both university graduates and mid-level technicians and skilled
workers, who can be employed in industrial installations and services
of different kinds. The Mariel Special Development Zone—and also
other areas of the country—could receive major investments that would
implement the strategy discussed above.*

An important issue is the pending claims resulting from the nation-
alizations of U.S. properties in Cuba, with a value estimated at seven
billion dollars. The resolution of this problem should be viewed in the
context of the Cuban demand for compensation for economic damages
from the blockade, valued at 116.8 billion dollars, according to data
provided on September 9, 2014, at the UN by Cuban deputy foreign
minister Abelardo Moreno.[37]

The new U.S. policy toward Cuba will stimulate other countries' investments. However, even if the blockade is lifted quickly, U.S. trade,
tourism, and investment will not produce positive results immediately,
because they will have to fit into Cuba's economic strategy, which
should quickly adapt to these new realities.

In summary, Cuba will have to reconfigure its reform project and
development agenda, in order to overcome internal mechanisms that
reproduce unsatisfactory approaches and replace them with innovative
ideas and practices. It would be a mistake to maintain a siege mentality,
without this implying that Cuba should not remain alert.

Defense and Security

Direct collaboration on defense and security continues to be focused on
Guantánamo and actions countering illegal migration.

It is well known that Cuba has been a victim of terrorist activities
organized by the U.S. government and perpetrated by its agencies, especially the CIA. These include numerous attempts on Fidel Castro's life.
Furthermore, since the beginning of the revolution a total of approximately seven thousand attacks have been carried out against the island,
including the Bay of Pigs (Playa Girón) invasion and the bombing of

---

* Alabama's Cleber company, owned by businessmen Horace Clemmons and Saul Beren-
thal, has become the first U.S. company authorized to establish its tractor assembly and
manufacturing plant in Cuba's Special Development Zone in Mariel, producing for sale on
the island and for export.

the Cubana Airlines plane in 1976 in which seventy-six civilians aboard lost their lives. These acts of terrorism cost the lives of 3,478 people and inflicted permanent injuries on another 2,099, as already noted.

The reestablishment of relations between the two countries offers a wide range of possibilities for agreements of different kinds in the areas of defense and security. Cuba's ability to deal with humanitarian and natural disasters and to protect the environment has been demonstrated during the recent humanitarian crisis in Haiti after the 2010 earthquake. The Cuban system of civil defense involves the armed forces, scientific institutions, the media, and social organizations that guarantee a maximum level of security and a minimum loss of human lives.

Although there is no bilateral treaty on *drug trafficking*, both countries' agencies involved in countering it have collaborated occasionally on specific matters. The U.S. agencies (the Drug Enforcement Administration [DEA], the coast guard, the navy, intelligence agencies, and the FBI) that deal with this issue have been interested in a formal agreement with Cuba, but U.S. policy has so far prevented them from reaching one such as those negotiated with other Caribbean countries.

In the area of relations between the *armed forces*, Cuba's position has been to promote "agreements that provide confidence to all countries regarding use of the sea and air spaces that surround them." A preliminary list of specific plausible areas for bilateral and multilateral cooperation would include preventive protection against natural disaster; environmental monitoring, especially of toxic substances in the Caribbean waters, nuclear materials, and epidemics; coastal protection; legal and community-based management of pollutants; protection of air and maritime security, saving the lives of illegal migrants, and prevention of piracy and hijacking; surveillance and interception of drug trafficking; military contacts to improve relations and mutual cooperation, trust-building measures in relation to military maneuvers, and information exchange; and sports, historical, cultural and academic encounters, and exchange of military delegations.[38]

Especially sensitive areas—some already noted in the previous paragraph—in which important agreements could be reached once relations have been restored include the following.[39]

Traditional Security

The hostility, asymmetry, and proximity of the United States have made it necessary for Cuba to develop a deterrent strategy based on armed forces that are small but have excellent combat capabilities. This means that the cost of an invasion of Cuba would be unsustainable in the context of the Cuban strategy of a "war of the whole people," despite the possibility of some limited, initial successes by the aggressor. What happened in Iraq confirms this perception.

Guantánamo

Cuba has reiterated that it considers the treaty establishing a U.S. naval base in Guantánamo to be illegal, but it has insisted that it will seek the return of this territory through diplomatic negotiations. Havana has not cashed the checks that the United States issues to "pay" rent on the land. In debates over the status of the detainees in Guantánamo, as a result of the global war on terror, Washington has recognized that Cuba holds true sovereign power over the territory. Both countries have taken measures to build mutual trust in the area surrounding the base and have even carried out joint training exercises for cases of natural disaster such as fires, hurricanes, and pandemics. The restoration of relations creates possibilities for important progress on this issue.

Migration

This is one of the most conflictive security issues in the relationship. Cuba has traditionally been a source of emigrants to the United States. Washington has wielded the migration issue as an instrument in its aggressive policy toward Cuba. Migration crises have occurred in 1965, 1980, and 1994 due to the U.S. policy of stimulating illegal emigration from Cuba, officially established by the Cuban Adjustment Act of 1966. In 1994 and 1995, the two countries signed mutual migration agreements establishing that twenty thousand permanent immigrant visas would be granted annually to Cuban citizens, in order to allow a regular, legal migratory flow controlled by both governments. Under this agreement, cooperation between the Cuban border guards and U.S. Coast Guard has contributed to safe navigation in the Florida Straits. But Washington's refusal to suspend or rescind the Cuban Adjustment Act makes it difficult to effectively implement the agreements.

Terrorism

We have already noted how the CIA promoted covert action against the island. The most recent actions were bombs in Havana hotels in 1999.

When the attacks on the Twin Towers and the Pentagon occurred, the Cuban government condemned them and offered its broad support to the U.S. government, offering medical assistance and opening Cuban air space and airports to planes from the United States or other countries that needed to make a forced landing. Cuba has attempted to stop terrorist acts that Cuban counterrevolutionaries have organized with impunity, on U.S. territory. It sent agents (the Cuban Five) to penetrate terrorist groups there, but they were arrested and received long prison sentences, while the notorious terrorist Luis Posada Carriles enjoys impunity. The reestablishment of relations will undoubtedly allow significant progress toward cooperation in this troubled area.

Hemispheric Security

Cuba does not participate in the current mechanisms of hemispheric security and has aligned itself with countries that criticize the United States for redeploying the Fourth Fleet, the agreement with Colombia to establish seven military bases on its territory, the coup in Honduras, and the presence of thousands of U.S. troops in Haiti.

Political-Economic Stability and Security

Ever since the triumph of the revolution, "the U.S. has carried out a policy replete with elements of subversion and destabilization directed against Cuba: economic sanctions to produce 'hunger, desperation and the overthrow of the government' financing and training of the opposition; media campaigns by way of stations such as Radio Martí and TV Martí; etc. This policy has not succeeded in toppling the government or destabilizing the country."[40]

Environment

1. *Climate change and disasters.* Public policies on the environment in both countries address climate change issues such as extreme events (hydro-meteorological, seismic, etc.), loss of biodiversity, and damage to the basic life-support systems of land (desertification, erosion, etc.) and water (aquifer salinization, drought, etc.). Given the proximity between the two countries, cooperation is key when it comes to environmental accidents (spills and chemical accidents).[41]

2. *Meteorological cooperation.* Despite their differences, cooperation between Cuba and the United States in the meteorological area has

involved information exchange between their specialized centers
(the National Hurricane Center in Florida and the Cuban Meteorological Institute).[42]

3. *Extreme events*. The Haiti earthquake of 2010 brought up the possibility and necessity of joint action in cases of regional emergency.
Cuba authorized opening its air space to U.S. planes that transported
emergency aid to Haiti, and the two governments maintained contact
on matters related to providing aid.[43]

Given Cuba's proximity, its stability should be a matter of great concern for the U.S. government, since uncontrolled migration to Florida
could be quite harmful. The restoration of relations could certainly
contribute to Cuba's stability by promoting its economic development.

To summarize, "if the United States has the technology, military
power, money, weapons and equipment, strategic lift, command and
control capabilities, and so much else to offer on a wider cooperative
effort . . . Cuba has the medical staff, experience, inter-American and
wider international legitimacy, geographical position, and political will
to make the most of these resources."[44]

Clearly, diplomatic relations between the two countries will enhance
all these possibilities of collaboration in areas such as defense and security.

Public Health

In regard to emerging diseases, pandemics, and plagues, both countries
develop pharmaceuticals and vaccines from which they can mutually
benefit.

Cuba and the United States have been able to collaborate through the
Pan American Health Organization (PAHO). The World Health Organization (WHO) has recognized Cuba's achievements in medicine on
more than one occasion.* On various occasions, the Centers for Disease
Control and Prevention (CDC) in Atlanta has cooperated with Cuban
authorities in the treatment of epidemics such as dengue fever and
polyneuritis. Keeping in mind that the PAHO has identified the Cuban
health system as one of the best in the region, and given the importance

---

* Cuba is the first country in the world to eliminate HIV and syphilis transmission from
mother to child, according to a WHO June 30, 2015, press release.

of this issue in the U.S. domestic agenda—prioritized by the Obama administration—the existing ties could be expanded. An example is the aid to victims of the Haiti earthquake, in which Cuba and the United States engaged in sustained dialogue at the foreign ministerial level to coordinate assistance. In addition, "the idea of the family doctor is in common use on both sides of the divide, as is the idea of preventive and community medicine. Mass education programs implemented on the Island about HIV/AIDS and drug consumption as well as the role of community and youth activists are experiences of mutual interest."[45]

Science, Culture, and Sports

Despite the aggressive U.S. policy toward Cuba, important scientific, academic, artistic, and intellectual exchanges and sports events have occurred for decades, and Cuba has achieved global leadership in all these areas. In sports, the island's long history of success in the Olympics as well as the Pan American and Central American Games offers fertile ground for collaboration. Presumably, as a result of the July 20 reestablishment of relations, the United States will agree that Cuban professionals in these areas can fulfill U.S. contracts without breaking their ties with the island; and similarly, the Cuban government will allow its workers in these areas to be hired without losing their ability to return home normally when they decide to do so. Thus, the exchange will be productive and will benefit both countries and their citizens.[46]

NOTES

1. "El 17D: Secuencias y consecuencias."
2. R. Hernández, "Intimate Enemies."
3. Gutiérrez, "Republican Case."
4. "Obama Gives the Castro Regime," *Washington Post*.
5. Obama, "Statement by the President."
6. Obama, "Interview by Candy Crowley."
7. R. Castro, "Statement by the Cuban President."
8. R. Castro, "Statement by Army General Raúl Castro Ruz."
9. Ibid.
10. R. Castro, "Statement by the Cuban President."
11. Obama, "Statement by the President."
12. R. Castro, "Statement by the Cuban President."

13. Wallerstein, "Cuba and the United States."
14. LeoGrande, "El 17D: Secuencias y consecuencias."
15. F. Castro, "For My Federation of University Students."
16. Ibid.
17. Jacobson, "Press Availability."
18. Ibid.
19. J. Vidal, "Cuba Wants."
20. Ibid.
21. A. Hernández, "Venezuela Is Not a 'National Security Threat.'"
22. Legañoa, "Cuba y EE.UU. conversarán."
23. Obama, "Statement by the President."
24. Obama, "Presidential Letter."
25. R. Castro, "Letter from Raúl Castro."
26. "Statement by the Revolutionary Government," *Granma*.
27. Ibid.
28. Univisionnoticias, "Exclusiva Encuesta en Cuba."
29. Obama, "Statement by the President."
30. Obama, "Executive Order."
31. Rodríguez Parrilla, "Canciller Bruno Rodríguez."
32. R. Castro, "We Must Call upon All."
33. LeoGrande, "5 Things Cuba Can Do."
34. Mesa-Lago, "Normalización de relaciones."
35. Lynch, "Estimaciones de escenarios económicas," 44.
36. Rodríguez, "Las relaciones económicas."
37. Trotta, "Cuba Estimates Total Damage."
38. R. Hernández, "Intimate Enemies," 24.
39. Alzugaray, "Cuba's National Security."
40. Ibid., 66.
41. Alzugaray, "La seguridad nacional."
42. Ibid.
43. Fernández, "Temas para una Posible Agenda."
44. Klepak, "Cuba-U.S. Cooperation," 89.
45. R. Hernández, "Intimate Enemies," 23.
46. Lutjens, "The Subject(s) of Academic"; Martínez Reinosa, "Academic Diplomacy."

Conclusion

The December 17 announcement of negotiations and the subsequent July 20 reestablishment of diplomatic relations took place in a context of changes in Cuba and the United States as well as in the international and geopolitical arenas that were favorable for Cuba. These include growing global multipolarity, despite U.S. military hegemony; the strength of the postneoliberal governments in Latin America and the Caribbean that challenge U.S. hegemony; talks with the European Union to eliminate the "Common Position"; Cuba's role in hosting and mediating talks between the Colombian government and the FARC; an almost unanimous UN vote against the blockade; Cuba's hosting of meetings of the CELAC and the Caribbean Community (CARICOM); worldwide recognition of the role of Cuban health-care personnel in the fight against Ebola; the so-called updating of the economic model in Cuba and the reforms that Raúl Castro is implementing; demographic changes in the Cuban exile community, in which young people overwhelmingly support Obama's new policy; the emergence of new political and economic actors in both the U.S. and Miami power and business structures as well as in American society as a whole that support restoring relations (including U.S. and Cuban American businesspeople and U.S. politicians, both Democrats and Republicans); consensus at the U.S. and global level on the failure of the blockade as a policy to overthrow the island's government; and the political agreement between

President Obama and Hillary Clinton on the need to change political strategy toward Cuba.*

However, there is a pronounced asymmetry between Cuba and the United States as actors in the negotiation process, which is why many analysts claim that Cuba benefits more from restoring relations, despite the significant benefits that this entails for U.S. "soft power" and its image in the region and globally.

Cuba established clear limits in its negotiating position, such as not accepting a loss of sovereignty or giving up key values, such as social justice and the redistribution of wealth. The United States is merely extending to Cuba the same status it has accorded to China and Vietnam for many years, without differentiating it from the more moderate (Brazil, Argentina, and Uruguay) or radical (Venezuela, Bolivia, Ecuador, and Nicaragua) projects that challenge U.S. hegemony in the region.

Moreover, the concept of "normalization" does not mean the same thing for Cuba as it does for the United States. For the Cuban government and society, normalization presumes that relations between the two countries will be based on the principles of international law and the UN Charter. However, the United States still has not clarified what steps it is prepared to take, once relations are restored, to "normalize" them.

Obama's new policy toward Cuba involves changes in strategy and tactics but not in objectives. The measures adopted tend to favor "civil society"—the private and not the public—without relaxing the pressure on the government. It was always assumed that relations would be restored and embassies opened once the blockade had been lifted, as occurred with Vietnam. However, under the new strategy, lifting the blockade was left for a second step of "normalization" subsequent to reestablishing relations, one clearly conditioned on how Cuba responded to other U.S. interests under negotiation.

Obama's December 17 speech contained a strategy and agenda identifying the key points of the policy change toward the island. This was appropriate for him and not the Cuban president because it was not Cuba that had severed relations, engaged in an aggressive policy, and refused to negotiate differences. At his July 1, 2015, press conference,

---

* See in "Cuba y Estados Unidos" contributors' observations and especially those of Aurelio Alonso, Juan Valdes Paz, Esteban Morales, Roberto Veiga, Lenier Gonzalez, and Jorge Dominguez.

in conjunction with the announcement that relations would resume on July 20, Obama once again called on Congress to lift the embargo.

In Obama's December 17 speech, the issues he discussed referred not to U.S. foreign policy but to Cuban domestic policy. Raúl Castro referred only to foreign policy issues for both countries; he did not propose any domestic changes in U.S. society, nor did he condition the course of negotiations on this, as did Obama.

Just as President Obama recognized the failure of U.S. policy toward Cuba, the Cuban leadership is aware that restoring relations would have a very positive effect on the island's economy, which is going through a difficult period due to lack of foreign investment and the crisis its main ally, Venezuela, is experiencing, due to the sharp drop in oil prices. This calls into question the possibility of Venezuela continuing its significant social programs and maintaining its economic relationship with Cuba on the existing, very favorable terms for the island.

The mutual decision announced on December 17 by Obama and Raúl Castro to open talks and the July 20 restoration of relations will trigger significant debate and polarization in the U.S. political system, in U.S. society, among Cuban Americans, and among Cuban migrants globally. There are also different visions of this process within Cuban society and even in the government itself. Constructing consent through dialogue as equals will not be an easy task.

Both countries' governments will surely pursue strategies of seeking agreements in the least conflictive areas—even strengthening existing agreements—while gradually working to resolve more thorny issues, without the negotiating parties giving up their interests and principles.

Canada, which has invested millions on the island and carried out an active diplomacy that engages with the public sector and civil society, could offer the United States a constructive model of relations with Cuba.

The complexity of the process of resolving differences between the two countries is not limited to those related to restoring and normalizing relations. While this process goes forward, policies must promote reunification between Cubans on the island and those who have emigrated, and between those who embraced the socialist project and those who abandoned or even fought against it but now agree to work together to create spaces for dialogue.

The good news is that the Cuban and U.S. people have never experienced the same degree of separation and hostility as their governments, as shown by the wide-ranging two-way exchange of tourists, athletes, scientists, academics and intellectuals, and artists of various kinds.

Reestablishing relations presents complex problems and contradictions for the island's government. For example, could Cuban Americans make major investments in Cuba, while Cuban businesspeople on the island continue to be restricted to small businesses in restaurants and housing rentals? Will it be possible for Cubans living on the island, if they obtain funding, to create large industrial, service, or other kinds of companies? Will the political system not require major changes as it undergoes the transition from being under attack to normal relations? This does not imply that the United States should dictate the changes that need to occur in different areas, but they certainly must be made, especially since the era of the historic leadership, whose unquestionable merits give them special legitimacy, will soon come to an end because of their age.[1]

Once restored, and even normalized, Cuban-U.S. relations will still experience tensions and contradictions, resulting from the imperial geopolitics and the messianic attitudes of U.S. leaders, in the context of an overwhelmingly asymmetric, David-versus-Goliath correlation of forces. Cuba, meanwhile, cannot give up policies that strengthen it, nor renounce its commitment to an international order that would correct existing imbalances through a culture of peace.

To summarize, this book has described two eras in Cuban-U.S. relations. The first lasted from the nineteenth century until the victory of the Cuban Revolution, and the second, from that victory in 1959 to the present.

During the first era, the United States always viewed Cuba not as a separate country with a right to independence but as something it desired and was entitled to possess in order to become complete as a nation and fulfill its "Manifest Destiny," with Cuba falling like "ripe fruit" into its lap. This perception of rightful ownership was based on the island's geographic location on the United States' southern border. Through its intervention in 1898, the United States prevented what had almost become a reality: Cuba winning its independence from Spain and taking its place among the other Latin American and Caribbean countries.

Thanks to conditions created by the neocolonial system, including the Platt Amendment in the first Cuban Constitution and "reciprocal trade" treaties, the United States turned the island into a nation with limited sovereignty in which it carried out multiple military interventions. It supported the Machado and Batista dictatorships, which faithfully served its interests in domination. These tyrannies led to two revolutions, one in 1933—thwarted by the United States—and the one in 1959, which they could not prevent, nor overthrow once it came to power.

The Cuban Revolution of 1959, which was the reaction against a U.S-supported dictatorship, quickly guaranteed social equality to the Cuban people, through policies to eradicate poverty, create full employment, and provide health and education. It accomplished all this while the most powerful country on earth was attempting to destroy the revolution. The island achieved full sovereignty, citizens were treated with the dignity they were entitled to, and Cuba became a symbol of resistance for the world. Eleven U.S. administrations could not prevent this despite unceasing efforts to subdue Cuba through armed invasions, covert operations, and the blockade intended to overthrow the island's revolutionary government and obstruct its economic development.

Now a new era has begun, a product of the negotiation process begun on December 17 that culminated in reestablishing diplomatic relations on July 20. This constitutes fertile ground for fruitful collaboration based on mutual respect. For example, cooperation could occur in areas where Cuba can contribute to scientific knowledge such as medicine, biotechnology, and the environment and in others where the United States leads, such as telecommunications and electronics, to mention just a few. Cuba has a highly educated, skilled population; the United States has know-how for innovation, production, and productivity.

The close enemies can now meet as friends on the common ground that has always united them: affinity and friendship between two peoples. Cuba has long loved U.S. culture, and the United States has always enjoyed the weather, music, cigars, and the friendliness of the Cubans.

We hope that the relationship between these two governments and societies can quickly make the transition from close enemies to friends, distant at first, but increasingly closer, as the requisites for true normalization are met and the powerful ties between the two societies flourish.

NOTE

1. See López Segrera, *La Revolución Cubana*.

Chronology

CUBA BEFORE THE REVOLUTION (1510–1959)

1510–1899	Spanish colonial domination of Cuba.
1898–1902	The United States intervenes in Cuba in a war that the Cubans had almost won after thirty years of struggle—with brief interruptions—against Spanish colonialism.
1902–1906	The pseudo-republic is born, in which the U.S. government establishes a neocolonial regime through Cuba's first president Tomás Estrada Palma.
1906–1909	The second U.S. intervention occurs, and Cuba is ruled by U.S. officials appointed as governors.
1909–1913	Elected government is restored under Liberal Party president José Miguel Gómez.
1912–1925	The government of Conservative Party president Mario G. Menocal is associated with U.S. investors in the sugar industry and serves as a more faithful tool of their interests than does Gómez.
1921–1925	Presidency of Alfredo Zayas, originally a Liberal, gains power with Conservative Party support.
1925–1933	Gerardo Machado is elected president and soon becomes a dictator.

1933–1934   The revolution of 1933 occurs, but the division among different revolutionary forces, among other factors, allows the U.S. government to overthrow it with the help of its main local ally, Fulgencio Batista.

1934–1944   Batista is the strongman of Cuban politics. Between 1934 and 1940, as commander of the armed forces, he controls several presidents as puppets. He serves as president between 1940 and 1944.

1944–1952   The Cuban Revolutionary Party (Authentic), characterized by administrative corruption and support from antilabor gangsterism, holds power under two presidents: Ramón Grau (1944–1948) and Carlos Prío (1948–1952). The Prío government unleashes a fierce persecution against the labor movement, which was led by communists.

1952–1959   Batista takes power through a coup d'état. His dictatorship involves even greater surrender to the United States than the Authentic governments. Following the coup, Fidel Castro begins to organize the struggle against him. The assault on the Moncada barracks on July 26, 1953, is its first major action, and it culminates victoriously on January 1, 1959, after the guerrilla campaign of the Sierra Maestra Mountains (1956–1959).

CUBAN-U.S. RELATIONS (1959–2015)

1959

January 1   The U.S. government welcomes and offers political asylum to human rights violators who flee Cuba after the victory of the revolution.

July 24   President Eisenhower signs legislation authorizing him to suspend assistance to any country that expropriates U.S. property but fails to "discharge its obligations under international law" to provide just compensation within six months.[1]

1960

March 4	The French ship *La Coubre* explodes in the port of Havana due to sabotage.
March 17	The president of the United States orders the director of the CIA, Allen Dulles, to start preparing an armed force of Cuban exiles to invade Cuba.
September 13	Cuba nationalizes U.S. companies and banks.
October 20	The United States decrees the embargo of exports to Cuba, initiating the trade blockade.
December 19	After the United States announces the definite end of Cuban sugar imports, a joint Soviet-Cuban communiqué reaffirms the Soviet Union's "complete support in maintaining Cuban independence against unprovoked aggression."[2]

1961

January 3	The U.S. government severs diplomatic relations with the revolutionary government of Cuba.
January 20	John F. Kennedy assumes the presidency of the United States.
April 17	An army of more than 1,500 counterrevolutionary Cubans, organized, trained, equipped, and financed by the CIA, launches the Bay of Pigs (Playa Girón) invasion.
April 24	President Kennedy admits U.S. responsibility for the failed mercenary Bay of Pigs invasion.

1962

February 3	President Kennedy issues a proclamation imposing a total embargo on trade between the United States and Cuba.
March 24	The U.S. Treasury Department prohibits the importation into the United States of any product produced all or in part in Cuba.
October 22	President Kennedy decrees a naval and economic blockade against Cuba, put into effect on October 23, thus initiating the so-called October Crisis, also known as the Missile Crisis.

1963

February 6	The U.S. government announces that merchandise financed by the United States cannot be transported in ships that trade with Cuba.
July 8	The U.S. government decides to freeze Cuban-owned assets in that country and to prohibit financial transactions with Cuba.
November 22	President John F. Kennedy is assassinated in Dallas, Texas.
November 23	Lyndon Baines Johnson assumes the presidency.
December 17	CIA saboteurs, using underwater demolition techniques similar to those used in World War II, mine a navy patrol boat docked in the south dock of the Bay of Siguanea, south of the Isle of Pines. Three Cuban sailors are killed, and eighteen are injured in the explosion.

1964

January 22	Secretary of state Dean Rusk urges U.S. allies to stop trading with Cuba and states that such commerce could frustrate the efforts to reduce the communist threat from Cuba.
February 15	Secretary of state Dean Rusk states that although some U.S. consumers as private citizens might decide to boycott products from companies that trade with Cuba, the U.S. government did not plan to organize such a consumer boycott.
February 18	The U.S. State Department announces that it has suspended military aid to Great Britain, France, and Yugoslavia for trading with Cuba, while it will keep aid to Spain and Morocco at current levels until they report what measures they have taken regarding their trade with Cuba.

1965

April 8	Cuba discovers and deactivates a spy and sabotage network headed by Baptist pastor Herbert Gaudill.

April 25   The U.S. militarily intervenes in Santo Domingo in the Dominican Republic. Cuba requests an urgent meeting of the Security Council to consider the U.S. aggression.

1966

November 2   The United States approves the Cuban Adjustment Act that legalizes illegal immigrants from Cuba who reach its shores and offers them other benefits.

1967

July 31   The First Latin American Solidarity Conference is inaugurated in Havana. Six CIA agents who had infiltrated the country are presented before journalists and delegates to the conference.

September 22   The XII Meeting of Consultation of the Organization of American States (OAS) meets in Washington and adopts new anti-Cuba resolutions.

1969

October 31   President Nixon describes his new doctrine against Cuba and Latin America as "a mature partnership."[3]

1969–1971   The U.S. government engages in new counterrevolutionary plans against Cuba, principally the Torriente Plan, named for a Cuban exile in Miami who advocated another invasion by armed exiles.

1970

May 10   Eleven Cuban fishermen are kidnapped by the Miami-based, paramilitary counterrevolutionary organization Alpha 66.

September   An artificial crisis erupts about supposed Soviet nuclear submarines in Cienfuegos.

1971

February 25   In a foreign policy report to Congress, President Nixon maintains his aggressiveness toward Cuba.

September   At a congressional session, the chairman of the Senate
                    Foreign Relations Committee, William Fulbright, in-
                    troduces Senate Resolution 160 to review U.S. policy
                    toward Cuba.

1973

January   In a report, twelve Republican representatives ask to
                    lift the blockade and normalize relations with Cuba.
February 15   Cuba and the United States sign the agreement on
                    airline and maritime hijacking and other offenses that
                    requires the United States to enforce the law of neu-
                    trality and reduce support for the counterrevolution.
                    From this date, the CIA begins promoting attacks
                    against Cuban diplomatic missions abroad and against
                    Cuban civilian aircraft.
October 5   Secretary of state Henry Kissinger proclaims a "new
                    dialogue" with Latin America under pressure from
                    Latin American countries that support Cuba.[4]

1974

April   Canadian and Argentine subsidiaries of U.S. compa-
                    nies flout the economic blockade imposed on Cuba,
                    and the State Department is forced to approve the
                    license "as an exception."

1975

During 1975   The U.S. government begins to consider the possi-
                    bility of changing its policy toward Cuba. Thus, the
                    U.S. press reports that until November talks between
                    officials of the two countries analyze possibilities for
                    subsequent agreements and negotiations. Counter-
                    revolutionary and CIA activities deescalate during this
                    year, as does the tone of U.S. government rhetoric.
December   President Ford states that the Cuban government's
                    sending combat forces to Angola destroys any oppor-
                    tunity for better relations with Cuba.

1976

March 23   Kissinger declares that "we are opposed—we cannot accept—any further Cuban military adventures. . . . What we will do in concrete circumstances I do not think I should say under present conditions."[5]

1977

January   President Carter ratifies Gerald Ford's decision to suspend reconnaissance flights over Cuba and to authorize Cubana Airlines aircraft to fly over U.S. territory.

September 1   Simultaneous ceremonies at the Swiss embassy in Havana and the Czech embassy in Washington inaugurate the Interests Sections of the United States and Cuba, respectively.

1978

January   Talks are held between representatives of the U.S. Coast Guard and Cuban border guards to cooperate on issues of mutual interest.

September   President Carter orders the resumption of spy flights over Cuban territory.

November–   Important contacts take place between the Cuban gov-
December   ernment and representatives of the Cuban community abroad. As a result, the Cuban government decides to allow members of the community to visit Cuba and frees many counterrevolutionary prisoners.

Throughout   Members of Congress continue to visit Cuba, U.S.
1978   prisoners are freed, and U.S. citizens and their families leave the country.

1979

September   Coinciding with the beginning of the Sixth Summit of the Non-Aligned Movement in Cuba, another major artificial crisis develops over the alleged presence of a Soviet combat brigade in Cuba.

1980

The Carter administration resumes the policy of encouraging illegal departures from Cuba.

January   Presidential candidate Ronald Reagan tells CBS that the United States should impose a naval blockade of Cuba as a countermeasure to the Soviet invasion of Afghanistan.

April   Events at the Peruvian embassy in Havana, when thousands of Cubans enter to seek permission to emigrate, generate a major anti-Cuba campaign in the media. The Cuban government allows free emigration from the port of Mariel.

November 4   Reagan is elected president of the United States.

December 17   The Second Congress of the Cuban Communist Party organizes national defense under the concept of "war of the whole people" with the creation of the Territorial Troop Militias (MTT).

1981

November 5   Reagan administration secretary of state Alexander Haig requests the Defense Department to develop plans for a possible blockade of Nicaragua or actions directed at Cuba, including naval exercises, a show of air power, quarantine, or even stronger action, all directed at halting the supply of arms to El Salvador.

December 4   At the OAS General Assembly in St. Lucia, Haig denounces a "systematic campaign of increasing interference" by Cuba in Central America.[6]

1982

January   The State Department continues the campaign to link Cuba with drug trafficking. Reagan, Haig, Thomas Enders, and Myles Frechette make aggressive statements.

1983

July 26   In a speech on the anniversary of the Moncada assault, Fidel Castro says he is in favor of a negotiated settlement with the United States to end the conflicts in Central America. He reiterates this to U.S. journalists on July 28.

October 25   The United States invades Grenada.

1984

December 14   Cuba and the United States sign migration agreements. Fidel Castro characterizes the agreements as "a constructive and positive fact" in his speech that same day but reiterates, "we should not neglect our defense."[7]

1985

May   Migration agreements between Cuba and the United States are suspended.

1987

February 3   The chairman of the Senate Foreign Relations Committee, Claiborne Pell, says he supports normalizing relations between the United States and Cuba.

November 20   Cuba and the United States decide to resume the 1984 Migration Agreement, suspended since May 1985.

1988

May–
December   Quadripartite meetings are held among delegations from Angola, Cuba, South Africa, and the United States (as mediator), reaching an agreement to the conflict in South-West Africa in December.

1989

December 20   The United States invades Panama and overthrows and detains President Noriega.

1990

February   After the electoral defeat of the Sandinistas in Nicaragua (following the U.S. invasions of Grenada in

October 1983 and of Panama in December 1989), the U.S. government makes overthrowing the Cuban Revolution its next objective.

1992

June   The U.S. Congress approves the Torricelli Act that intensifies the economic and financial blockade of Cuba. It authorizes cutting off aid to governments that provide loans and other services to Cuba and penalizes American companies whose subsidiaries in third countries trade with Cuba.

October 23   President Bush signs the Torricelli Act, which provokes strong opposition to the law from Canada, Mexico, and other Latin American countries (Argentina, Venezuela, and Uruguay).

1994

April 22–24   The conference "The Nation and Emigration" takes place in Havana between representatives of the Cuban government and Cuban citizens in exile, both in the United States and in Europe. Both sides agree to continue the dialogue underway about issues of mutual interest and to create a Permanent Commission to deal with issues related to emigration.

July 13   The tugboat *13 de marzo* is sunk after being seized by a group of people who wanted to immigrate to the United States illegally.

August 5   An antigovernment uprising takes place in Cuba on the Havana Malecón, where hundreds of people demonstrate in protest of the economic crisis. The protest is suppressed in a few hours.

August 13   The rafter (*balsero*) crisis explodes after Fidel Castro announces at a press conference that he will open Cuba's border, leading to the mass exodus of people from the island.

September 9   Cuba and the United States sign a new migration agreement that provides for U.S. acceptance of twenty thousand legal immigrants per year in exchange for Cuba's prevention of mass emigration by sea.

1995

May 2   A joint Cuban-U.S. declaration is issued, broadening the reach of the September 9 migration agreements. The United States agrees to return all illegal immigrants to Cuba.

July 26   President Fidel Castro strongly criticizes U.S. policy toward Cuba, which represents a hardening of his position, and warns about the corruption generated by the economic reforms.

1996

February 24   Cuban air force fighters shoot down two civilian planes from the anti-Castro group Brothers to the Rescue, based in southern Florida.

March 12   The U.S. Congress passes the Helms-Burton Act. President Clinton tightens the blockade with this law that applies internationally. Months later, he suspends the application of Title III, which provides that the United States can sanction companies investing in property confiscated by the Cuban regime.

1999

December 2   The Elián González crisis intensifies when his grandmothers ask the Cuban foreign minister, Felipe Pérez Roque, to intercede with the U.S. government to return the boy, held in the United States since November 25.

2000

April 22	Elián is rescued and returned to his father after a raid by federal agents that took him by force from the home of his paternal great uncle Lázaro González in Miami.
June 28	Elián returns to Cuba accompanied by his father.
December 28	Clinton authorizes the sale of food and medicine to Cuba if it pays in cash.

2001

A Miami court finds the Cuban Five, imprisoned since 1998, guilty of espionage for trying to prevent terrorist activities against Cuba.

2002

May	Dissident Oswaldo Payá presents the Varela Project, asking parliament for a referendum on reforms to the political and economic system.

2003

March	The government imprisons seventy-five dissidents accused of receiving money from the United States to subvert order in Cuba.

2004

May 6	The U.S. government presents a report from the Commission for Assistance to a Free Cuba that includes plans for major restrictions on travel to Cuba and more aid for dissidents to try to accelerate the end of the Fidel Castro regime.
May 21–25	The third "Nation and Emigration" conference is held in Havana, at which attendees agree on criticism of the hardening of U.S. policy.

2005

November 17   Fidel Castro warns in a speech that there is a possibility that the revolution could self-destruct as a result of its internal errors.

2006

July 31   President Fidel Castro issues a proclamation announcing his temporary retirement because of pending surgery.

2007

April 19   Cuba blames the United States for freeing the anti-Castro terrorist Luis Posada Carriles.

July 26   In a major speech, Raúl Castro declares, "We need to bring everyone to the daily battle against our own errors." This precipitates a great national debate about the Cuban model of socialism and proposals for change. "We need to bring everyone to the daily battle against the very errors which aggravate objective difficulties derived from external causes."[8]

2008

February 19   Fidel Castro resigns. After he announces that he will not accept reelection to the presidency, five days later his brother Raúl is elected president of the Council of State.

2009

May 31   Cuba accepts the U.S. proposal to resume talks about migration and indicates its willingness to discuss cooperation in the areas of terrorism, drug trafficking, and natural disasters.

December 3   U.S. contractor for USAID, Alan Gross, is detained in Havana for counterrevolutionary activities.

2010

From the beginning of the year, a fierce media campaign is unleashed against Cuba because of prisoner Orlando Zapata's death as a result of his hunger strike and the beginning of a hunger strike by another prisoner, Guillermo Fariñas.

June   After talks first with the Cuban Catholic Church and then with Spain's minister of foreign relations, the Cuban government agrees to free by November 2010 fifty-two prisoners still jailed of the seventy-five detained in the spring of 2003 for crimes against state security.

July 14   Fidel Castro appears in public for the first time since becoming ill in July 2006. He warns of a possible nuclear war by the United States and Israel against Iran.

2011

January 14   President Obama announces the liberalization of travel restrictions and remittances to Cuba.

2013

July 19   Talks about migration issues between Cuba and the United States resume in Washington.

2014

December 17   Barack Obama and Raúl Castro announce in Washington and Havana the decision to initiate a negotiation process to reestablish relations between the two countries.

2015

January 21–22   The first of four rounds of negotiations on restoring diplomatic relations is held in Havana.

February 27	The second round of negotiations takes place in Washington.
March 16	The third round of negotiations occurs in Havana.
April 11	Presidents Raúl Castro and Barack Obama have a one-hour-and-twenty-minute meeting at the Summit of the Americas, after making speeches the previous day.
May 21–22	The fourth round of negotiations is held in Washington.
July 1	Presidents Raúl Castro and Barack Obama exchange letters in which they announce that on July 20 diplomatic relations will be reestablished and embassies will open in Cuba and the United States.
July 20	Diplomatic relations between Cuba and the United States are reestablished, and respective embassies open in Havana and Washington.

NOTES

1. Vandevelde, *U.S. International Investment Agreements*, 17; Eisenhower, "Statement by the President upon Approval of Bill," 171.

2. Blasier, "Elimination of United States Influence," 71.

3. Nixon, "Remarks at the Annual Meeting of the Inter-American Press Association."

4. Kissinger, "Toast: A Western Hemisphere Relationship," 1.

5. Kissinger, "Secretary Kissinger's News Conference," 469.

6. Haig, "Feature: OAS General Assembly."

7. F. Castro, "Castro Discusses Immigration Agreement."

8. R. Castro, "Speech by the First Vice-President of the Councils of State and Ministers."

Bibliography

Aja Díaz, Antonio. "U.S.-Cuba: Emigration and Bilateral Relations." In *Debating U.S.-Cuban Relations: Shall We Play Ball?* edited by Jorge I. Domínguez, Rafael Hernández, and Lorena G. Barbería, 201–17. New York: Routledge, 2012.

Albright, Madeleine. "U.S. Announces Steps to Increase Humanitarian Aid to Cuba." CNN Interactive, March 29, 1998. http://www.cnn.com.

Alonso, Aurelio. "Continuidad y transición: Cuba en el 2007." *Le Monde Diplomatique*, Colombia ed., April 2007, 1–6.

Alzugaray, Carlos Treto. "Cuba cincuenta años después: continuidad y cambio político." *Temas* no. 60 (October–December 2009). http://temas.cult.cu.

———. "Cuba's National Security vis-à-vis the United States." In *Debating U.S.-Cuban Relations: Shall We Play Ball?* edited by Jorge I. Domínguez, Rafael Hernández, and Lorena G. Barbería, 52–71. New York: Routledge, 2012.

———. "La actualización de la política exterior cubana." *Política Exterior*, no. 161 (September–October 2014). http://www.politicaexterior.com.

———. "La seguridad nacional de Cuba frente a los Estados Unidos: conflicto y ¿cooperación?" In *¡Play Ball¡ Debatiendo las relaciones Cuba-Estados Unidos*, edited by Jorge I. Domínguez and Rafael Hernández, 168–70. Ediciones Temas Habana, 2015.

Amuchástegui, Domingo. "Neither Gray Quinquennium nor Black Decade, but Endless Struggle for Ideas and Diversity in Revolutionary Cuba." *CubaNews*, July 30, 2007. http://www.walterlippmann.com.

Arbesú, José, and Germán Sánchez. "Las relaciones EU-Cuba bajo la administración Carter." *Estados Unidos, perspectiva latinoamericana*, no. 5 (January–June 1979): 275–93. http://biblat.unam.mx.

Arboleya, Jesús. "Cuba: una batalla inusual en Washington." *Progreso Semanal*, January 23, 2015. http://progresosemanal.us.

———. *La revolución del otro mundo*. Havana: Editorial Ciencias Sociales, 2008.

Attwood, William. *The Twilight Struggle: Tales of the Cold War*. New York: Harper & Row, 1987.

Báez, Luis. *El mérito es estar vivo*. Havana: Prensa Latina, 2005.

Barbería, Lorena G. "U.S. Immigration Policies toward Cuba." In *Debating U.S.-Cuban Relations: Shall We Play Ball?* edited by Jorge I. Domínguez, Rafael Hernández, and Lorena G. Barbería, 180–200. New York: Routledge, 2012.

Binder, David. "Cuba Sanctions, Imposed in 1964, Lifted by O.A.S." *New York Times*, July 30, 1975. http://www.nytimes.com.

Blasier, Cole. "The Elimination of United States Influence." In *Revolutionary Change in Cuba*, edited by Carmelo Mesa-Lago, 43–80. Pittsburgh: University of Pittsburgh Press, 1971.

Bolton, John R. "Beyond the Axis of Evil: Additional Threats from Weapons of Mass Destruction." Lecture to the Heritage Foundation, Washington, DC, May 20, 2002. http://www.heritage.org.

Borón, Atilio. *América Latina en la geopolítica imperial*. Havana: Editorial de Ciencias Sociales, 2014.

Brundenius, Claes. "Revolutionary Cuba at 50: Growth with Equity Revisited." *Latin American Perspectives* 36, no. 2 (2009): 31–49.

Brzezinski, Zbigniew. *Strategic Vision: America and the Crisis of Global Power*. New York: Basic, 2012.

Buell, Raymond Leslie, and Foreign Policy Association, Commission on Cuban Affairs. *Problems of the New Cuba*. New York: Foreign Policy Association, 1935.

Bush, George H. W. "Another Perspective." *Miami Herald*, February 27, 1992, 19A. Reprinted in *Bangor Daily News*, February 28, 1992. https://news.google.com.

———. "Remarks to Religious and Ethnic Groups in Garfield, New Jersey." July 21, 1992. 41 George Bush Presidential Library and Museum Public Papers, College Station, TX. https://bush41library.tamu.edu.

Bush, George W. "Remarks Announcing the Initiative for a New Cuba." Administration of George W. Bush 2002, May 20, 2002, p. 822. https://www.gpo.gov.

———. "Remarks on Cuba, October 10, 2003." Public Papers of George W. Bush, July 1–December 31, 2003, p. 1294. Washington, DC: Government Printing Office. https://books.google.com.

Carranza, Julio, Luis Gutiérrez Urdaneta, and Pedro M. Monreal González. *Cuba: la reestructuración de la economía. Una propuesta para el debate*. Havana: Editorial de Ciencias Sociales, 1995.

Castro, Fidel. "Castro Discusses Immigration Agreement with U.S." Castro Speech Data Base, University of Texas Latin American Network Information Center, LANIC, December 15, 1984. http://lanic.utexas.edu.

———. "Comparecencia del presidente Fidel Castro ante la Televisión Cubana y las ondas internacionales de Radio Habana Cuba, el día 11 de agosto de 1994." Havana: Consejo de Estado, August 11, 1994. http://revolucioncu bana.cip.cu.

———. "Discurso . . . en la Clausura del IV Congreso del Partido Comunista de Cuba, Santiago de Cuba, October 14, 1991." Portal Cuba. Accessed November 23, 2016. http://www.cuba.cu.

———. "For My Federation of University Students Classmates." *Granma*, January 26, 2015. http://en.granma.cu.

———. "Histórica carta de Fidel a Celia June 5, 1958." Reprinted in *Diario Granma*, June 5, 2013. http://www.granma.cu.

———. "History Will Absolve Me." October 16, 1953. Castro Internet Archive. Accessed November 25, 2016. https://www.marxists.org.

———. "Interview of Fidel Castro." House of Representatives, Select Committee on Assassinations, Washington, DC. CTKA. Accessed November 23, 2016. http://www.ctka.net.

———. "Reflexiones." *Granma Internacional*, 2007–2015.

———. "Varadero News Conference." Castro Speech Data Base, University of Texas Latin American Network Information Center LANIC Data Base, May 26, 1994. http://lanic.utexas.edu.

Castro, Raúl. "Discursos de Raúl." *Granma*. Accessed November 23, 2016. http://www.granma.cu.

———. "Letter from Raúl Castro—Re-establishing Diplomatic Relations and Permanent Diplomatic Missions—June 30, 2015." White House, Press Office, Washington, DC, July 1, 2015. http://www.whitehousepressbriefings .com.

———. "Presidential Letter to Obama, December 17, 2014." White House, Office of the Press Secretary, Briefing Room, July 1, 2015. https://www .whitehouse.gov.

———. "Speech by the First Vice-President of the Councils of State and Ministers, Army General Raúl Castro Ruz, at the Main Celebration of the 54th Anniversary of the Attack on Moncada and Carlos Manuel de Céspedes Garrisons, at the Major General Ignacio Agramonte Loynaz Revolution Square in the City of Camagüey, July 26th, 2007, 'Year 49 of the Revolution.'" *Granma*, July 26, 2007. http://www.granma.cubaweb.cu.

———. "Statement by Army General Raúl Castro Ruz, First Secretary of the Central Committee of the Communist Party of Cuba and President of the Councils of State and of Ministers at the Closing Ceremony of the Fourth Session of the Eighth Legislature of the National People's Power Assembly

Held at Havana's Conference Center on December 20, 2014, 'Year 56 of the Revolution,'" December 20, 2014. Portal Cuba. Accessed November 24, 2016. http://www.cuba.cu.

———. "Statement by the Cuban President." December 17, 2014. Google Docs. Accessed November 24, 2016. https://docs.google.com.

———. "We Must Call upon All the Peoples and Governments of Our America to Mobilize and Be Alert in Defense of Venezuela." *Granma*, March 18, 2015. http://en.granma.cu.

Clinton, William J. "Preface to the Report Entitled 'Support for a Democratic Transition in Cuba.'" January 28, 1997. Public Papers of the Presidents of the United States, William J. Clinton, 1997, book 1, p. 89. U.S. Government Publishing Office. https://www.gpo.gov.

———. "Statement on Cuban Independence Day." May 20, 1994. Public Papers of the Presidents of the United States, William J. Clinton, January–July 31, 1994, p. 965. Google Books. https://books.google.com.

Commission for Assistance to a Free Cuba. "Report to the President, May 2004." U.S. Department of State, Washington, DC, 2004. USAID. http://pdf .usaid.gov/pdf_docs/PCAAB192.pdf.

———. "Report to the President, July 2006, by Condoleezza Rice and Carlos Gutiérrez." U.S. Department of State, Washington, DC, 2006. Council on Foreign Relations. http://www.cfr.org.

Committee of Santa Fe et al. *A New Inter-American Policy for the Eighties*. Washington, DC: Council for Inter-American Security, 1980.

———. *Santa Fe II: A Strategy for Latin America in the Nineties*. Washington, DC: Council for Inter-American Security, 1988.

Constitución de la República de Cuba. Havana: Editorial Orbe, 1976.

"Cuba y Estados Unidos: los dilemas del cambio, Debate." Sinpermiso, January 18, 2015. http://www.sinpermiso.info.

Daniel, Jean. "I Was There When Castro Heard the News about JFK." *New Republic*, December 7, 1963. https://newrepublic.com.

———. "Unofficial Envoy: An Historic Report from Two Capitals." *New Republic*, December 14, 1963. https://ratical.org.

"Declaraciones: Declaración de Santiago de Cuba." *Política Internacional*, no. 7 (1964).

"Declaraciones: Primera Declaración de Habana." Havana: Proyección Internacional de la Revolución Cubana, 1975.

"Declaraciones: Segunda Declaración de Habana." Havana: Proyección Internacional de la Revolución Cubana, 1975.

"Desafíos económicos de Cuba." *Cuba Posible*, no. 3 (2014). http://www .cubaposible.net.

"Document 56, Prime Minister Castro's 'Five Points' Letter to UN Secretary General U Thant." In *The Cuban Missile Crisis: A Chronology of Events*,

October 28, 1962—around noon. National Security Archive. Accessed November 24, 2016. http://nsarchive.gwu.edu.

Domínguez, Jorge I. "Reshaping the Relations between the United States and Cuba." In *Debating U.S.-Cuban Relations: Shall We Play Ball?* edited by Jorge I. Domínguez, Rafael Hernández, and Lorena G. Barbería, 32–51. New York: Routledge, 2012.

Domínguez, Jorge I., Rafael Hernández, and Lorena G. Barbería, eds. *Debating U.S.-Cuban Relations: Shall We Play Ball?* New York: Routledge, 2012.

Eisenhower, Dwight D. "Statement by the President upon Approval of Bill Amending the Mutual Security Act of 1954." Public Papers of the Presidents of the United States, Dwight D. Eisenhower, 1959, p. 171. Google Books. https://books.google.com.

"El 17D: Secuencias y consecuencias." *Catalejo* el blog de *Revista Temas* (interviews with William LeoGrande, Pedro Monreal, Jorge Domínguez, Carlos Alzugaray, Meg Crahan, Jesús Arboleya, and Frank O. Mora y Rafael Hernández). January 5, 2015. http://temas.cult.cu.

Espina Prieto, Mayra. "Mirar a Cuba hoy: cuatro supuestos para la observación y seis problemas nudos." *Temas*, no. 56 (2008). http://temas.cult.cu.

Feinberg, Richard. *Soft Landing in Cuba? Emerging Entrepreneurs and Middle Classes*. Washington, DC: Brookings, 2013.

Fernández, Armando. "Temas para una Posible Agenda Ambiental entre Cuba y Estados Unidos." Unpublished manuscript, 2015.

Florida International University y Cuban Research Institute (FIU-CRI). *2014 FIU Cuba Poll: How Cuban Americans in Miami View U.S. Policies toward Cuba*. Miami: FIU Cuban Research Institute, 2014. https://cri.fiu.edu.

Frank, Marc. "Cuba Flirts with Free Press." AFP, Havana, February 23, 2015.

Franklin, Jane. *Cuban Foreign Relations: A Chronology*. New York: Center for Cuban Studies, 1984.

"Full Text of the Ostend Manifesto." Aix-la-Chapelle, Prussia, October 15, 1854. HistoryofCuba.com. Accessed November 24, 2016. http://www.historyofcuba.com.

García Márquez, Gabriel. "Cuba en Angola: Operación Carlota." *Proceso* (Cuba), January 1977, 6–15.

Gleijeses, Piero. *Misiones en Conflicto: La Habana, Washington y África, 1959–1976*. Havana: Editorial Ciencias Sociales, 2002.

Granma. "Statement by the Revolutionary Government." July 1, 2015. http://en.granma.cu.

Guanche, Julio César. *El poder y el proyecto. Un debate sobre el presente y el futuro de la revolución en Cuba*. Santiago, Cuba: Editorial Oriente, 2009.

Guevara, Ernesto ("Che"). *El Che en la Revolución Cubana*. 7 vols. Havana: Editorial José Martí, 2013.

Gutiérrez, Carlos M. "A Republican Case for Obama's Cuba Policy." *New York Times* Op-ed, June 23, 2015. http://www.nytimes.com.

Habel, Janette. *Ruptures à Cuba: le castrisme en crise.* Paris: La Brêche, 1989.

Haig, Alexander. "Feature: OAS General Assembly . . . Secretary's Address, Dec. 4, 1981." *Department of State Bulletin* 82, no. 2058 (January 1982). https://archive.org.

Hakim, Peter. "Los malos hábitos pueden descarrilar las negociaciones Cuba-EEUU." *Infolatam*, March 3, 2015. http://www.infolatam.com.

Hernández, Alicia. "Venezuela Is Not a 'National Security Threat' after All, Obama Says." Vice News, April 10, 2015. https://news.vice.com.

Hernández, Rafael. "Cuban Dissidents: Allies of US Policy or a Hindrance?" *Huffington Post*, April 19, 2015. http://www.huffingtonpost.com.

———. "Intimate Enemies: Paradoxes in the Conflict between the United States and Cuba." In *Debating U.S.-Cuban Relations: Shall We Play Ball?* edited by Jorge I. Domínguez, Rafael Hernández, and Lorena G. Barbería, 9–31. New York: Routledge, 2012.

Hernández, Rafael, and Jorge I. Domínguez, ed. *¡Play Ball! Debatiendo las relaciones Cuba-Estados Unidos.* CD-ROM. Havana: Ediciones Temas, 2015.

Ibarra, Jorge. "El experimento cubano." In *Diez Años de la Revista Casa de las Américas, 1960–1970.* Havana: Casa de las Américas, 1970.

Jacobson, Roberta. "Press Availability with Assistant Secretary Roberta Jacobson." U.S. Department of State, Havana, January 23, 2015. http://www.state.gov.

Jiménez, Guillermo. *Las empresas de Cuba 1958.* Havana: Editorial Ciencias Sociales, 2004.

Kennedy, Robert F., Jr. "Opinion: JFK's Secret Negotiations with Fidel." Inter Press Service, January 5, 2015. http://www.ipsnews.net.

———. "Opinion: Sabotaging U.S.-Cuba Détente in the Kennedy Era." Inter Press Service, January 6, 2015. http://www.ipsnews.net.

———. "Opinion: We Have So Much to Learn from Cuba." Inter Press Service, December 30, 2014. http://www.ipsnews.net.

Kissinger, Henry. "Secretary Kissinger's News Conference at Dallas, March 23." *Department of State Bulletin* 74, no. 1920 (April 12, 1976): 469–75. https://www.fordlibrarymuseum.gov.

———. "Toast: A Western Hemisphere Relationship of Cooperation, April 5, 1973." In *The Inter-American Relationship.* Reprint from *Department of State Bulletin.* http://www2.mnhs.org.

———. *World Order.* New York: Penguin, 2014.

Klepak, Hal. "Cuba-U.S. Cooperation in the Defense and Security Fields: Where Are We; Where Might We Be Able to Go?" In *Debating U.S.-Cuban Relations: Shall We Play Ball?* edited by Jorge I. Domínguez, Rafael Hernández, and Lorena G. Barbería, 72–91. New York: Routledge, 2012.

Kornbluh, Peter. "Terrorism and the Anti-Hijacking Accord in Cuba's Relations with the United States." In *Debating U.S.-Cuban Relations: Shall We Play Ball?* edited by Jorge I. Domínguez, Rafael Hernández, and Lorena G. Barbería, 92–99. New York: Routledge, 2012.

Landau, Saul, and Nelson P. Valdés. "Una revisión de la política hacia Cuba: ¿No son suficientes 54 años de fracaso?" *Cuba Debate*, April 8, 2013. http://www.cubadebate.cu.

Legañoa, Jorge. "Cuba y EE.UU. conversarán sobre las misiones diplomáticas." *CubaSi*, May 21, 2015. http://www.cubasi.cu.

LeoGrande, William M. "El 17D: Secuencias y consecuencias." Interview with *Catalejo, Revista Temas* blog, January 5, 2015. http://temas.cult.cu.

———. "5 Things Cuba Can Do to Speed the Normalization of Relations with the United States." *Huffington Post*, March 5, 2015. http://www.huffington post.com.

———. "Normalizing Relations with Cuba: The Unfinished Agenda." *Newsweek*, January 30, 2015. http://www.newsweek.com.

LeoGrande, William M., and Peter Kornbluh. *Back Channel to Cuba: The Hidden History of Negotiations between Washington and Havana.* Chapel Hill: University of North Carolina Press, 2014.

López Segrera, Francisco. *Cuba Cairá?* Petrópolis, Brazil: Vozes, 1995.

———. *Cuba: capitalismo dependiente y subdesarrollo (1510–1959).* Havana: Casa de las Américas, 1972.

———. *Cuba: cultura y sociedad (1510–1985).* Havana: Editorial Letras Cubanas, 1989.

———. *Cuba después del colapso de la URSS (1989–1997).* Mexico City: UNAM, Centro de Investigaciones Interdisciplinarias en Humanidades, 1998.

———. "The Cuban Revolution: Historical Roots, Current Situation, Scenarios, and Alternatives." *Latin American Perspectives* 38, no. 2 (2011): 3–30.

———. *Cuba: política exterior y revolución (1959–88).* Havana: Instituto Superior de Relaciones Internacionales (ISRI), 1988.

———. *Cuba sans l'URSS (1989–1995).* Lille, France: Presses Universitaires, Septentrion, 1997.

———. "El diferendo Cuba-EE.UU: Una visión desde La Habana." *Nueva Sociedad*, no. 99 (January–February 1989): 58–70.

———. *La administración Reagan y la Cuenca del Caribe.* Havana: Ciencias Sociales, 1989.

———. *La política de la administración Reagan hacia Cuba: antecedentes y posible evolución.* Havana: UNEAC, 1987.

———. *La política exterior de Cuba hacia América Latina (1959–88).* *Cuadernos del CENDES*, September–December 1988.

———. *La Revolución Cubana: propuestas, escenarios, alternativas.* Barcelona: El Viejo Topo, 2010.

———. *Raíces históricas de la Revolución Cubana (1868–1959)*. Havana: UNEAC, 1980.

López Segrera, Francisco, and Francisco José Mojica. *¿Hacia dónde va el mundo? Prospectiva, megatendencias y escenarios latinoamericanos*. Barcelona: El Viejo Topo, 2015.

López Segrera, Francisco et al. *De Eisenhower a Reagan: la politica de Estados Unidos contra la revolucion Cubana*. Havana: Ciencias Sociales, 1987.

Lutjens, Sheryl. "On the Left with the Cuban Revolution." *Latin American Perspectives* 36 (March 2009): 5–16.

———. "The Subject(s) of Academic and Cultural Exchange: Paradigms, Powers, and Possibilities." In *Debating U.S.-Cuban Relations: Shall We Play Ball?* edited by Jorge I. Domínguez, Rafael Hernández, and Lorena G. Barbería, 218–36. New York: Routledge, 2012.

Lynch, Tim. "Estimaciones de escenarios económicas alternativos de Cuba." In *Cuba, el Caribe y el Post Embargo*, edited by Alejandra Liriano de la Cruz, 23–47. Santo Domingo, Dominican Republic: FLACSO, 2005.

Martí, José. "Letter from José Martí to Manuel Mercado, May 18, 1895." Mexi-Can, May 28, 2013. http://www.mexi-can.org.

———. *Obras Completas*. Havana: Dirección de Cultura, 1973.

Martínez Heredia, Fernando. *El Corrimiento hacia el rojo*. Havana: Letras Cubanas, 2001.

Martínez Reinosa, Milagros. "Academic Diplomacy: Cultural Exchange between Cuba and the United States." In *Debating U.S.-Cuban Relations: Shall We Play Ball?* edited by Jorge I. Domínguez, Rafael Hernández, and Lorena G. Barbería, 237–55. New York: Routledge, 2012.

Mayor Zaragoza, Federico. *Un Mundo Nuevo*. Barcelona: Ediciones UNESCO, Galaxia Gutenberg, 2000.

Mesa-Lago, Carmelo. "Normalización de relaciones entre EEUU y Cuba: causas, prioridades, progresos, obstáculos, efectos y peligros." Working Paper No. 6. Real Instituto Elcano, Madrid, May 8, 2015. http://www.realinstitu toelcano.org.

Monereo, Manuel, Miguel Riera, and Juan Valdés Paz, ed. *Cuba: construyendo futuro*. Barcelona: El Viejo Topo, 2000.

Monreal González, Pedro. "El problema económico de Cuba." En Espacio Laical, Suplemento Digital, no. 28 (April 2008). http://www.espaciolaical.org.

Monroe, James. Annual Message to Congress (Monroe Doctrine). December 2, 1823. Internet Archive. Accessed November 24, 2016. http://www.archive.org.

Morales Domínguez, Esteban. Commentaries. http://estebanmoralesdomin guez.blogspot.com.

Morales Domínguez, Esteban, and Gary Prevost. *United States–Cuban Relations: A Critical History*. Lanham, MD: Lexington, 2008.

Naím, Moisés. "Los autogoles de la superpotencia." *El País*, May 10, 2015.

Neugebauer, Rhonda L. "Payment for Services Rendered: US-Funded Dissent and the 'Independent Libraries Project' in Cuba." *World Libraries* 13, no. 1 (Spring 2003): 23.

Nixon, Richard. "Remarks at the Annual Meeting of the Inter-American Press Association." October 31, 1969. American Presidency Project. Accessed November 24, 2016. http://www.presidency.ucsb.edu.

Obama, Barack. "Executive Order: Blocking Property and Suspending Entry of Certain Persons Contributing to the Situation in Venezuela." White House, Office of the Press Secretary, Washington, DC, March 9, 2015. https://www.whitehouse.gov.

———. "Interview by Candy Crowley." *State of the Union with Candy Crowley,* CNN, December 21, 2014. http://cnnpressroom.blogs.cnn.com.

———. "Presidential Letter: Re-establishing Diplomatic Relations and Permanent Diplomatic Missions." White House, Office of the Press Secretary, Washington, DC, June 30, 2015. https://www.whitehouse.gov.

———. "Remarks by the President at the Summit of the Americas Opening Ceremony." White House, Office of the Press Secretary, April 17, 2009, Port of Spain, Trinidad and Tobago. https://www.whitehouse.gov.

———. "Statement by the President on Cuba Policy Changes." White House, Office of the Press Secretary, Washington, DC, December 17, 2014. https://www.whitehouse.gov.

———. "Statement by the President on the Re-establishment of Diplomatic Relations with Cuba." White House, Office of the Press Secretary, Washington, DC, July 1, 2015. https://www.whitehouse.gov.

Oficina Nacional de Estadística e Información (ONE). *Anuario Estadístico de Cuba 2013.* Accessed November 24, 2016. http://www.one.cu.

———. *Panorama económico y social de Cuba 2014.* Accessed November 24, 2016. http://www.one.cu.

"On Celebrating the Cuban Revolution." *Latin American Perspectives* 36, no. 1 (2009): 5–17.

Partido Comunista de Cuba. "VI Congreso." *Cuba Debate*, April 16, 2011. Accessed November 24, 2016. http://www.cubadebate.cu.

Perera Gómez, Eduardo. "The European Union and Its Role in U.S.-Cuban Relations." In *Debating U.S.-Cuban Relations: Shall We Play Ball?* edited by Jorge I. Domínguez, Rafael Hernández, and Lorena G. Barbería, 100–120. New York: Routledge, 2012.

Pérez, Louis A., Jr. *Cuba in the American Imagination.* Chapel Hill: University of North Carolina Press, 2008.

Pérez, Villanueva, et al. *Miradas a la economia cubana.* Havana: AECID: Editorial Caminos, 2009.

Ramírez Cañedo, Elier, and Esteban Morales Domínguez. *De la confrontación a los intentos de normalización: la política de los Estados Unidos hacia Cuba.* Havana: Editorial de Ciencias Sociales, 2014.

Ramonet, Ignacio, and Fidel Castro. *Fidel Castro: biografía a dos voces*. Madrid: Debate, 2006.

Revolutionary Government. "Statement, July 1, 2015." *Granma*, July 1, 2015. http://en.granma.cu.

Ritter, Archibald, R. M. "U.S.-Cuba Relations: The Potential Economic Implications of Normalization." In *Debating U.S.-Cuban Relations: Shall We Play Ball?* edited by Jorge I. Domínguez, Rafael Hernández, and Lorena G. Barbería, 139–59. New York: Routledge, 2015.

Roa García, Raúl. *Retorno a la alborada*. 2 vols. Santa Clara, Cuba: Universidad Central de las Villas, 1964.

Roa Kourí, Raúl. *En el Torrente*. Havana: Fondo Editorial Casa de las Américas, 2004.

Rodríguez, José Luis. "Las relaciones económicas entre Cuba y EEUU en un nuevo escenario." *Cuba Debate*, April 29, 2015. http://www.cubadebate.cu.

Rodríguez Parrilla, Bruno. "Canciller Bruno Rodríguez: en momentos en que se agrede a Venezuela Cuba siente que se le agrede también." *Aporrea*, March 14, 2015. http://www.aporrea.org.

———. "Speech by Bruno Rodríguez Parrilla, Minister of Foreign Affairs of the Republic of Cuba, at the United Nations General Assembly." ahora.cu, November 13, 2012. http://www.ahora.cu.

Sánchez, Germán. *Cuba y Venezuela*. Havana: Editorial José Martí, 2006.

Sánchez Egozcue, Jorge Mario. "U.S. Cuba Economic Relations: The Pending Normalization." In *Debating U.S.-Cuban Relations: Shall We Play Ball?* edited by Jorge I. Domínguez, Rafael Hernández, and Lorena G. Barbería, 160–79. New York: Routledge, 2015.

Sánchez Parodi, Ramón. *Cuba-USA: Diez tiempos de una relación*. Mexico City: Ocean Sur, 2011.

Serguera Riverí, Jorge. *Che Guevara: la clave africana*. Jaén, Spain: Líberman, 2008.

Smith, Wayne S. *The Closest of Enemies: A Personal and Diplomatic Account of U.S.-Cuban Relations since 1957*. New York: Norton, 1987.

Stone, Oliver, and Peter Kuznick. *The Untold History of the United States*. New York: Gallery Books, 2012.

Suárez Salazar, Luis. "The Cuban Revolution and the New Latin American Leadership: A View from Its Utopias." *Latin American Perspectives* 36, no. 2 (2009): 114–27.

———. "La proyección externa de la Revolución cubana." In *Cuba: construyendo futuro*, edited by Manuel Monereo, Miguel Riera, and Juan Valdés Paz, 331–62. Barcelona: El Viejo Topo, 2000.

Sweig, Julia E. *Cuba: What Everyone Needs to Know*. New York: Oxford University Press, 2009.

Taller Académico Cuba-Estados Unidos (TACE). *Oportunidades para las relaciones Cuba-Estados Unidos: Documento de Trabajo; propuestas para la colaboración en áreas de interés mutuo, noviembre 2012*. Buenos Aires: CRIES, 2013. http://www.academia.edu.

Trotta, Daniel. "Cuba Estimates Total Damage of U.S. Embargo at $116.8 billion." Reuters, September 9, 2014. http://www.reuters.com.

United Nations Development Programme. *United Nations Development Report 2014*. New York: Author, 2014.

Univisionnoticias. "Exclusiva Encuesta en Cuba: una Encuesta de Bendixen & Amandi Internacional para Univision Noticias y Fusion en colaboración con *The Washington Post*." April 2015. Univision Noticias. http://huelladigital .univisionnoticias.com/encuesta-cuba.

Valdés, Juan. *El Espacio y el límite: estudios sobre el sistema político cubano*. Havana: Instituto Cubano de Investigación Cultural Juan Marinello, 2009.

Valdés, Nelson P. "Revolutionary Solidarity in Angola." In *Cuba in the World*, edited by Cole Blasier and Carmelo Mesa-Lago, 87–117. Pittsburgh: University of Pittsburgh Press, 1979.

Vandevelde, Kenneth J. *U.S. International Investment Agreements*. New York: Oxford University Press, 2009.

Vidal, Josefina. "Cuba Wants U.S. to Cut Support of Anti-Castro Dissidents." *ABC 10 News*, January 24, 2015. http://www.local10.com.

Vidal, Pável. "La crisis bancaria cubana actual." Espacio Laical, June 2010. http://espaciolaical.org.

———. "El PIB cubano en 2009 y la crisis global." IPS-Economics Press Service, no. 9, Havana, May 15, 2009. Estudios Económicos Cubanos. Accessed November 24, 2016. http://www.cuba-economia.org.

Wallerstein, Immanuel. "Cuba and the United States Resume Relations: Happy New Year." *Commentary*, no. 392, January 1, 2015. Immanuel Wallerstein. http://iwallerstein.com.

Washington Post. "Castro Cautiously Welcomes Changes in U.S.-Cuba Policy." March 21, 1998. https://www.washingtonpost.com.

———. "Obama Gives the Castro Regime in Cuba an Undeserved Bailout." December 17, 2014. https://www.washingtonpost.com.

Wikipedia. "John L. O'Sullivan." Last updated October 14, 2016. https:// en.wikipedia.org.

Wood, Leonard. "Leonard Wood to Theodore Roosevelt, October 28, 1901." Theodore Roosevelt Center. Accessed November 24, 2016. http://www .theodorerooseveltcenter.org.

ARCHIVES

Archivo nacional, Havana
Archivos de la Revolución, Havana

Archivos de Salvador Vilaseca, Havana
Library of the University of California, Riverside Special Collections,
  especially the Ronald H. Chilcote and Saul Landau Archives

JOURNALS AND MAGAZINES

Bohemia, Havana
Boletín del Centro de Investigaciones de la Economía Mundial, Havana
Cahiers des Amériques latines, Paris
Cuadernos de Nuestra América, Centro de Estudios de América, Havana
Cuba Internacional, Havana
Cuban Studies, University of Pittsburgh
Cuba Socialista, Havana
Economía y Desarrollo, Havana
Ediciones COR, Havana
Ediciones DOR, Havana
Foreign Affairs, Washington, DC
Foreign Policy, Washington, DC
Gaceta de Cuba, Unión Nacional de Escritores y Artistas de Cuba,
  Havana
Gaceta Oficial de Cuba, Havana
Latin American Perspectives, University of California, Riverside
Memorias del Banco Nacional de Cuba, Havana
Nueva Sociedad, Caracas, Venezuela
Obra Revolucionaria, Havana, 1959–1965
Pensamiento Crítico, Havana, 1967–1970
Pensamiento Propio, CRIES
Politique étrangère, Paris
Problèmes d'Amérique Latine, Paris
Temas, Havana
Tricontinental, Havana

NEWSPAPERS

El Nuevo Herald, Miami
El País, Madrid

Granma, Havana
Granma International, Havana
International Herald Tribune
Juventud Rebelde, Havana
Le Monde, France
Le Monde Diplomatique, France
Newsweek
New York Times
Revolución, Havana
Trabajadores, Havana

WEBSITES

Cuba Debate, http://www.cubadebate.cu
El Nuevo Herald, http://www.elnuevoherald.com
Granma, http://www.granma.cubaweb.cu
Granma International, http://www.granma.cu/idiomas/ingles
Juventud Rebelde, http://www.juventudrebelde.cu
Kaos en la Red, http://www.kaosenlared.net
La Jiribilla, http://www.lajiribilla.cu
Latin American Perspectives, http://lap.sagepub.com/content/current
Rebelión, http://www.rebelion.org
Temas, http://www.temas.cult.cu
Theodore Roosevelt Center, http://www.theodorerooseveltcenter.org

Index

international law, 20, 88
International Monetary Fund (IMF), 52
international order, 3
international relations: 1979–1989, 31; in multipolar world order, 33–37; United States, Europe, and Japan, 31
Internet, 24, 25–26, 60, 73
interventionism, 41–43
Iran, 36, 61, 106
Iraq War, 23, 51
Israel, 36, 106

Jacobson, Roberta, 26, 62
January 26, 2015, 62
Japan, 31, 35
Jefferson, Thomas, 37–38
Johnson, Lyndon B., 13, 96
July 20, 2015 reestablishment of diplomatic relations, 1, 2, 11, 57, 65, 89, 107

Kennedy, John F., 12–13, 95, 96
Kennedy, Robert F. Jr., 12
Kerry, John, 26, 60
Kissinger, Henry, 98, 99
Kissinger Report, 33

land use, neocolonial, 7–8
Latin America: U.S. interventionism, 42–43
Latin America and the Caribbean (LAC), 30, 31, 47–48, 49, 52
Latin American Economic System (SELA), 30
Latin American Summits, 22–23
lawsuits, 20
leftist governments, 34
LeoGrande, William, 61, 74, 76
liberation movements, Cuban support for, 30, 32, 46, 47, 50
"linkage" policy, 18

Linowitz Reports, 14
Little War (1879–1880), 38
lobbying, 21

Machado, Gerardo, 7, 91, 93
Maduro, Nicolás, 75
mafia, anti-Cuban, 22
Mandela, Nelson, 57
Manifest Destiny, 38, 39, 90
Mariel port emigration, 49, 72, 100
Mariel Special Development Zone, 34, 80
Martí, José, 43
Marxist ideology, 8
McKinley, William, 38
Medina González, Marcelino, 65
Menges, Constantine, 48
Menocal, Mario G., 93
Mercado, Manuel, 43
metaphors, 38–41
meteorological cooperation, 83–84
Mexico, 37
Middle East, 35
migration policies, 4, 16, 62, 82, 101–3; accord of 1984, 15, 19, 101; "*balsero* (rafter) crisis" of August 1994, 18–19, 21, 51, 102; Mariel emigration, 49, 72, 100; visas, 14, 19–20, 48, 67, 71, 82
military provocations, 1983–1989, 14–15
Ministry of Foreign Relations (Cuba), 26, 62, 64
Monroe, James, 38
Monroe Doctrine, 38
Moreno, Abelardo, 80
multipolarity, 31, 33–37, 68
mutual perceptions, 29–53; 1959–1962, 29, 44–46; 1962–1970, 30, 46–47; 1970–1979, 30–31, 47–49; 1979–1989, 31, 49–50; 1989–2015, 31–33, 50–51;

professionals, 35–36, 72
Protestant Interreligious Foundation
   for Community Organization
   (IFCO)/Pastors for Peace, 17
public health, 84–85
Puerto Rico, 14, 42, 49
Putin, Vladimir, 34

Radio Martí, 14, 15, 16, 19, 23, 25
"rafter (*balsero*) crisis" of August
   1994, 18–19, 21, 51, 102
Reagan, Ronald, administration,
   14–15, 22, 31, 48, 49–50, 100
"reciprocity" treaties, 9
"reconcentration camps," 41
regional governments, 3
remittances, 21, 24, 60, 73, 78
Reports to the President (Plan Bush I
   and II), 23
Republic of Cuba, 42, 65–66
Republican Party, 17, 52, 58, 61
"the revolution betrayed" metaphor,
   44
Rice, Condoleezza, 24
ripe fruit theory, 38, 39, 40, 90
Rodríguez Parilla, Bruno, 25, 66, 75
Roosevelt, Theodore, 38, 41
Root, Elihu, 42
Rumsfeld, Donald, 23
Rusk, Dean, 46, 96
Russia, 16, 33, 34

Samper, Ernesto, 58
Sanchez, Celia, 44
Sante Fe II (Second Santa Fe
   Document), 15, 48
Schlesinger, Arthur, 12
science, culture, and sports, 85
security relations, 3
Senate Foreign Relations Committee,
   46, 101
September 11, 2001, 23, 823

Seventh Summit of the Americas, 24,
   58, 63, 69, 75, 76
Shannon, Thomas, 24
Sheritt International, 35
slavery, 6, 40
Smith, Wayne, 45
socialism, 91, 105; "actually
   existing," 32; market economy,
   34; new model, 12; Soviet model,
   9–10; updating of economic
   model, 2, 33, 61, 72, 87
Sorensen, Theodore, 12
South Africa, 30
South-West Africa (Namibia), 15,
   16, 101
sovereignty, Cuban, 2, 6, 29, 46, 52,
   58–60, 67, 74, 91
Soviet Union, 9, 32; Africa and,
   15–16; Cuban Missile Crisis
   and, 12–13; Czechoslovakia,
   invasion of, 9–10; détente, 48;
   dissolution of, 16, 18, 36, 50, 51,
   67; model of socialism, 9–10;
   reestablishment of relations, 1960,
   44–45; U.S.-Soviet agreements,
   1962, 30
Spain, 5, 20, 36
Spanish American War, 5–6, 40–41
Special Period, 10, 11, 51
Spooner, John Colt, 41
"Statement by the Revolutionary
   Government" (July 1, 2015), 66
Stevenson, Adlai, 13
subversion, U.S., 12, 23, 25, 32,
   45–46, 60, 66, 74, 83, 104, 2021
sugar production, 6, 7–8, 43, 93
Summit of the Americas (2009), 24,
   68–69, 75, 107

technology, 73
telecommunications, 17, 24, 79
Ten Years' War (1869–1878), 38, 40

About the Author

Francisco López Segrera was an official at UNESCO between 1994 and 2002, where he worked as, among other positions, director of the International Institute of Higher Education of UNESCO for Latin America and the Caribbean (IESALC). He was vice chancellor of the Advanced Institute of International Relations of Cuba (1980–1989), where he periodically teaches. He was a member of the UNESCO Forum on Higher Education (2002–2009), was an academic advisor (2004–2012), and is currently a consultant for GUNI (Global University Network for Innovation) and professor chair of UNESCO university administration of the Universidad Politécnica de Cataluña (UPC). He has also served as professor at the Centro de Pensamiento Estratégico y Prospectiva of the Universidad Externado de Colombia. He has been a visiting professor at more than fourteen universities in Latin America, Spain, the United States, Canada, France, and Africa and has presented papers at conferences at 120 universities in those and other countries including China, Austria, Russia, and Canada. Those universities include UNAM, Boston College, SUNY Binghamton, University of California Berkeley, Stanford, Oxford, University of California Riverside, Sorbonne, and Salamanca. He is the author of twenty-five books and dozens of articles translated into seven languages about prospective developments in international relations, among them *Cuba Cairá?* (1995); *Cuba sans l'URSS (1989–1995)* (1997); *Cuba después del colapso de la URSS (1989–1997)* (1998); *América Latina 2020: escenarios, alternativas y estrategias*, editor, coauthor, and coordinator with Daniel Filmus (2000);

América Latina y el Caribe en el siglo XXI: perspectiva y prospectiva de la globalización, coordinator and coauthor with Francisco José Moica, with preface by Federico Mayor Zaragoza and introduction by Immanuel Wallerstein (2004); *Escenarios Mundiales de la Educación Superior* (2006); *Educación Superior Internacional Comparada: escenarios, temas y problemas* (2010); *La Revolución Cubana: propuestas, escenarios, alternativas* (2010); and *¿Hacia dónde va el mundo? Prospectiva, megatendencias y escenarios latinoamericanos*, coauthored with Francisco Mojica (2015).